Contents

Table of Cases

Table of Statutes

Table of Statutory Instruments

Table of European Legislation

How to use this book

Welcome to this new edition of Routledge-Cavendish European Union Law Lawcards. In response to student feedback, we've added some new features to these new editions to give you all the support and preparation you need in order to face your law exams with confidence.

Inside this book you will find:

■ NEW tables of cases and statutes for ease of reference
■ Revision Checklists

We've summarised the key topics you will need to know for your law exams and broken them down into a handy revision checklist. Check them out at the beginning of each chapter, then after you have the chapter down, revisit the checklist and tick each topic off as you gain knowledge and confidence.

■ Key Cases

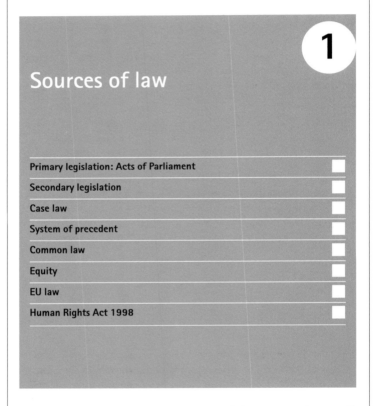

1

Sources of law

Primary legislation: Acts of Parliament	☐
Secondary legislation	☐
Case law	☐
System of precedent	☐
Common law	☐
Equity	☐
EU law	☐
Human Rights Act 1998	☐

We've identified the key cases that are most likely to come up in exams. To help you to ensure that you can cite cases with ease, we've included a brief account of the case and judgment for a quick aide-memoire.

■ Companion Website

HENDY LENNOX v GRAHAME PUTTICK [1984]

Basic facts

Diesel engines were supplied, subject to a *Romalpa* clause, then fitted to generators. Each engine had a serial number. When the buyer became insolvent the seller sought to recover one engine. The Receiver argued that the process of fitting the engine to the generator passed property to the buyer. The court disagreed and allowed the seller to recover the still identifiable engine despite the fact that some hours of work would be required to disconnect it.

Relevance

If the property remains identifiable and is not irredeemably changed by the manufacturing process a *Romalpa* clause may be viable.

At the end of each chapter you will be prompted to visit the Routledge-Cavendish Lawcards companion website where you can test your understanding online with specially prepared multiple-choice questions, as well as revise the key terms with our online glossary.

You should now be confident that you would be able to tick all of the boxes on the checklist at the beginning of this chapter. To check your knowledge of Sources of law why not visit the companion website and take the Multiple Choice Question test. Check your understanding of the terms and vocabulary used in this chapter with the flashcard glossary.

■ Exam Practice

Once you've acquired the basic knowledge, you'll want to put it to the test. The Routledge-Cavendish Questions and Answers provides examples of the kinds of questions that you will face in your exams, together with suggested answer plans and a fully-worked model answer. We've included one example free at the end of this book to help you put your technique and understanding into practice.

QUESTION 1

What are the main sources of law today?

Answer plan

This is, apparently, a very straightforward question, but the temptation is to ignore the European Community (EU) as a source of law and to over-emphasise custom as a source. The following structure does not make these mistakes:

■ in the contemporary situation, it would not be improper to start with the EU as a source of UK law;

■ then attention should be moved on to domestic sources of law: statute and common law;

■ the increased use of delegated legislation should be emphasised;

■ custom should be referred to, but its extremely limited operation must be emphasised.

ANSWER

European law

Since the UK joined the European Economic Community (EEC), now the EU, it has progressively but effectively passed the power to create laws which are operative in this country to the wider European institutions. The UK is now subject to Community law, not just as a direct consequence of the various treaties of accession passed by the UK Parliament, but increasingly, it is subject to the secondary legislation generated by the various institutions of the EU.

1

Sources of law

Understand why the European Communities were established
and how the European Union has developed ☐

Know the key features of the Treaties establishing the European
Communities and the European Union and the content of the
amending Treaties ☐

Have some knowledge of the main features of the Treaty of Lisbon
(yet to be ratified) ☐

Be able to identify and discuss the four main sources of
Community law ☐

SOURCES OF LAW

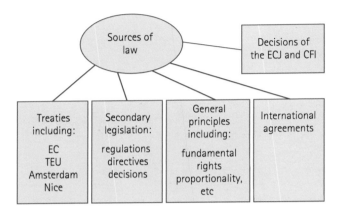

There are four sources of EU law:

- ■ law enacted by Member States which are the founding Treaties (primary legislation) and law enacted by the EC (secondary legislation);

- ■ general principles of law recognised by the European Court of Justice (ECJ);

- ■ international agreements with non-Member States.

- ■ decisions of the European Court of Justice (ECJ) and the Court of First Instance (CFI).

PRIMARY LEGISLATION
One of the main characteristics of the EU legal order is that it is based on a written constitution made up of the constitutive Treaties as follows:

ECSC Treaty (1951)
EC Treaty (1957)
EURATOM Treaty (1957)
Convention Relating to Certain Institutions Common to European
  Communities (1957)
Merger Treaty (1967)

First and Second Budgetary Treaties (1970 and 1975)
Treaties of Accession (1973, 1981, 1986, 1995 and 2003)
Single European Act (1986)
Treaty on European Union (1992)
Treaty of Amsterdam (1997)
Treaty of Nice (2001)

European Coal and Steel Community Treaty (ECSC)

Established by the Treaty of Paris in 1951, the purpose of the European Coal and Steel Community was to create a common market for coal and steel products.

The ECSC Treaty was the first of the constitutive Treaties. It exhibited a functionalist approach to integration, attempting to integrate economies sector by sector. A criticism of this approach is that it was an unnatural operation, as the integrated sector retained indissoluble links with other sectors of the economy which still had their national character. Its justification was that it was a first step, to be followed by integration of other sectors of the economy, toward the eventual integration of the whole economy.

An innovative feature of the ECSC Treaty was the creation of four supra-national institutions:

1 Council of Ministers – representing the Member States;
2 High Authority – intended as a supra-national executive, consisting of independent individuals rather than government representatives, empowered to take legally binding decisions and to procure funds, fix maximum and minimum prices for certain products and fine businesses in breach of competition rules;
3 Assembly – a parliament composed of delegates appointed by respective parliaments of the Member States;
4 Court of Justice – intended to review the legality of the Acts of the High Authority or, in some cases, businesses.

(Note: The ECSC lapsed in July 2002.)

European Atomic Energy Community Treaty (EURATOM)

Established by the Treaty of Rome 1957, the purposes of EURATOM were to create a specialist market for atomic energy and distribute it through the Community and to develop nuclear energy and sell surplus to non-Community States.

EURATOM had its own Commission (which was the equivalent to the ECSC's High Authority) and Council of Ministers, but shared an Assembly and Court of Justice with the ECSC and European Economic Community. EURATOM was another example of sectoral, or functional, integration.

European Economic Community Treaty (now the European Community)

The European Economic Community was established by a separate Treaty of Rome in 1957, and its name was amended by the Treaty on European Union (TEU). Its aim, as stated in the Preamble, was 'to lay the foundations of an ever closer union among the peoples of Europe'.

MEMBERSHIP

The original EEC was formed by six Member States: Belgium, France, (West) Germany, Italy, Luxembourg and the Netherlands. Since then the EEC (subsequently renamed EC) has expanded to include a further 21 countries: Denmark, Ireland and the UK (in 1973), Greece (1981), Portugal and Spain (1986), Austria, Finland and Sweden (1995), Cyprus, Czech Republic, Estonia, Hungary, Latvia, Lithuania, Malta, Poland, Slovakia and Slovenia (2004), Bulgaria and Romania (2007). Negotiations continuè with Turkey.`

The EEC had its own separate Commission and Council of Ministers but it shared an Assembly and Court of Justice with EURATOM and the ECSC.

The Treaty of Rome embodied a very different approach to integration from that of the ECSC and EURATOM Treaties. Whereas the latter attempted to integrate sector by sector, the EEC Treaty concentrated on types of activity rather than particular industries (with the exception of agriculture and transport), and aimed to ensure the effective functioning of the market together with free and fair competition. Another characteristic of the Treaty of Rome was that it laid down general principles, leaving it to the institutions to enact in detail. Policy making and regulation were also left to the institutions.

Timetables were laid down for the elimination of both mutual trade barriers and the common external tariff. Through these methods, the founders hoped to achieve economic integration, which was intended to be the forerunner of political integration. The Treaty was intended as a first step, to be followed by later Treaties which would build on the progress made.

Merger Treaty

The three different Communities had created three different sets of institutions, although they shared the same Assembly and Court of Justice. It became inconvenient to have three different sets of institutions, so a Merger Treaty came into force in 1967. The three Communities themselves did not merge, but the High Authority and two Commissions merged to form a single Commission, and the three Councils merged to form a single Council. Hartley, in *Foundations of European Community Law*, 5th edn, 2003, uses the analogy of three commercial companies with the same shareholders and same board of directors. In law, there are three legal persons; in reality, there is one.

The most important features of the Merger Treaty have been incorporated into the EC Treaty by the Treaty on European Union.

Single European Act (SEA)

Signed in 1986, the SEA was the first major amendment to the EC Treaty. It came about as a result of pressure for increased union and concern over increased competition from North America and the Far East. A major aim of the SEA was to speed up the decision making process through greater use of qualified majority voting, a system of weighted voting whereby Member States with larger populations receive more votes in the Council of Ministers than those States with smaller populations.

The SEA saw a widening of the process of European integration. This is illustrated by powers given to the EC in new areas. Whilst the original Treaty of Rome was principally concerned with integration of types of economic activity, the SEA granted powers to the EC for the co-ordination of economic and monetary policy and foreign policy. Both areas had been left out of the original Treaty. Other new areas included: social policy; powers to create a regional policy called 'economic and social cohesion'; environmental policy; and co-operation in research and technological development. The process of European integration could also be said to have been deepened, as well as widened, by the SEA.

The greater use of qualified majority voting meant that Member States could be out-voted and bound against their will. This represented a significant transfer of sovereignty from Member States to the European Community. Greater powers were also given to the European Parliament, an institution which is not under national control. The Commission, which is also outside national control, was given a central role in ensuring that the internal market was set up on time.

The major amendments were as follows:

- inauguration of the internal market programme for completion by 31 December 1992;

- introduction of qualified majority voting in the Council of Ministers for enactment of measures where they have as their object 'the establishment and functioning of the internal market';

- change in implementing powers of the Commission;

- creation of a co-operation procedure for enhanced consultative participation of the European Parliament in the legislative process;

- power of veto given to the European Parliament over the accession of new Member States and over the conclusion of agreements with associate States;

- recognition of the European Council as a formal organ of the European Community;

- authority granted to the Council of Ministers to create the Court of First Instance;

- co-operation in the field of foreign policy through European political co-operation;

- co-operation in economic and monetary policy;

- common policy for the environment;

- co-operation in research and technological development;

■ measures to ensure the economic and social cohesion of the Community;

■ harmonisation in the fields of health, safety, consumer protection, academic, professional and vocational qualifications, public procurement, VAT and Excise duties and frontier controls.

Treaty on European Union (TEU)

The next amendment to the EC Treaty was the Maastricht Treaty (officially known as the Treaty on European Union). The TEU created a European Union with three pillars: European Community, Common Foreign and Security Policy, and Justice and Home Affairs Policy.

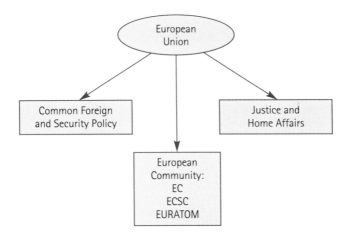

General principles

The Treaty on European Union has provisions on three matters of constitutional importance: human rights, subsidiarity and citizenship:

■ Art 6 (formerly Art F) of the TEU enshrines the existing practice that fundamental human rights are to be a general principle of Community law;

■ the principle of subsidiarity was introduced into EC law, in matters relating to the environment, by the SEA. It was made a general principle of EC law by virtue of the TEU. Article 5 of the EC Treaty provides that, in matters which are not within the Community's exclusive competence, the Community will

7

only take action if the scale of the proposed action means that it can be better achieved by the Community;

■ every national of a Member State is to become a citizen of the European Union (Art 17 of the EC Treaty).

Economic and monetary union

The Treaty sets out the procedure and timetable for creating economic and monetary union (EMU).

Other changes

The TEU introduced a number of other changes, including:

■ establishment of a Committee of Regions;

■ Court of Auditors becomes a Community institution;

■ greater powers for the European Parliament, with the introduction of a new legislative procedure.

Treaty of Amsterdam (ToA)

The Treaty of Amsterdam, which came into force in May 1999, was a consolidation, rather than an extension, of Community powers. It was also intended to prepare the Community for an expansion in membership, with the inclusion of Central and Eastern European States. A further aim was to make the European Union seem less remote to the citizens of Europe.

Common provisions

A principle of openness was added to the Treaty, so that decisions are taken 'as openly as possible' and as closely as possible to the citizen. Article 6 (formerly Art F) of the TEU, which enshrined the principle of fundamental human rights in the Treaty, has been amended. If the Council of the European Union finds a 'persistent and serious breach' by a Member State of the principles of fundamental human rights, the Council may suspend some of the State's rights under the Treaty, including voting rights.

Other changes

Other changes introduced by the ToA include the following:

■ Much of the third pillar of the European Union, the Justice and Home Affairs pillar, is incorporated into the EC Treaty. The third pillar now covers

Police and Judicial Co-operation in Criminal Matters (PJCC). The body of law, *acquis communautaire*, created by the Schengen Treaty 1985 which gradually abolishes border checks, is brought within the EU. The UK and Ireland are not bound by the Schengen *acquis* but can opt in whenever they wish to do so. Denmark has a partial opt-out from the Schengen *acquis*.

- There is an attempt to simplify the EC Treaty, which includes renumbering.

- The Community is given new tasks. The promotion of equality between men and women, protection and improvement of the environment, a high degree of competitiveness and 'sustainable' economic development are expressly stated to be Community goals.

- The Luxembourg Accords, which grant a Member State a right of veto if a decision affects one of its vital national interests, are enshrined in the Treaty. The right of veto had previously been a constitutional convention.

- New powers are given in the field of non-discrimination. The Community now has competence to combat discrimination in the fields of sex, racial or ethnic origin, religion or belief, disability, age and sexual orientation.

- A new title on employment has been added to the EC Treaty. Measures taken under this section are intended to support and complement national measures. The measures are confined to being 'soft law', ie, they are not legally binding.

- The co-decision procedure is amended and extended to new areas, thereby strengthening the role of the European Parliament.

- The Committee of Regions has the right to be consulted in a wider number of areas.

- The European Parliament is given the right to consult the Committee of Regions and the Economic and Social Committee, as well as the Council and the Parliament.

- The Community is given legislative power to combat fraud.

- A principle of flexibility is enshrined in the Treaty. This allows groups of Member States to integrate and co-operate further on specific issues when there is no agreement amongst all the Member States about the need for further integration or co-operation. It is possible for these groups of States to make use of the procedures, institutions and mechanisms laid down in the Treaty.

Treaty of Nice

In February 2001 the Treaty of Nice was signed. After ratification, it came into force in February 2003. The main points are as follows:

- Reweighting of votes during qualified majority voting (QMV) procedures in the Council of Ministers. More power is given to the larger nations: the UK, Germany, France, Italy and Spain.

- Use of QMV in the Council of Ministers is increased for reasons of speed and efficiency. Approximately 39 new policy areas no longer require a unanimous vote.

- A unanimous vote will still be required for legislation regarding taxation, social security, immigration, movement of professionals and foreign trade in culture.

- Groups of eight or more countries will be able to pursue further integration independently under a new 'reinforced co-operation' procedure.

The Charter of Fundamental Rights

In December 2000, during the Nice summit, a Charter of Fundamental Rights was approved by the governments of the EU's Member States. The document consists of 50 articles on a range of issues. It is essentially a consolidation of rights derived from a variety of pre-existing documents, such as the European Convention on Human Rights and the Community Charter of the Fundamental Social Rights of Workers (1989). Some of the key rights and freedoms in the Charter are right to life (Art 2); prohibition of torture and inhuman or degrading treatment or punishment (Art 4); prohibition of slavery and forced labour (Art 5); respect for private and family life (Art 7); freedom of thought, conscience and religion (Art 10); equality between men and women (Art 23); freedom of movement and of residence (Art 45).

The legal status of this Charter is not entirely clear – the Nice declaration specifically refrained from giving it binding legal force. However, this does not mean that its provisions have no relevance whatsoever. In several cases from 2001 onwards various Advocates General have referred to it during proceedings in cases pending before the ECJ (see Chapter 3). In *BECTU* (2001), for example, Advocate General Tizzano said:

> . . . in proceedings concerned with the nature and scope of a fundamental right, the relevant statements of the Charter cannot be ignored; in particular, we cannot ignore its clear purpose of serving, where its provisions so allow, as a substantive point of reference for all those involved – Member States, institutions, natural and legal persons – in the Community context.

The European Convention

At the European Council summit meeting in Laeken, Belgium in December 2001, it was agreed that the EU needed a constitution. You will probably agree that, with the EC/EU based on five Treaties from 1957, 1986, 1992, 1997 and 2001, actually finding, let alone understanding, EC law seems quite a daunting prospect. Officially, the idea of a Constitution is to make the principles and objectives of the EC/EU more accessible to its citizens. Cynics suggest that it is more than this – it is paving the way for a 'federal' Europe – a 'United States of Europe'.

Notwithstanding the political arguments, a body named the European Convention was set up in spring 2002 to start work on drafting a Constitution. The Convention team comprised 105 people representing the existing and prospective EU Member States and their Parliaments, the European Parliament and the Commission. It was chaired by the former French president Valéry Giscard d'Estaing. The Convention produced its final draft Constitution in May 2003. Key proposals include:

■ An elected president (elected by EU leaders that is) to serve as a figurehead for a period of 2½–5 years.

■ A foreign minister to conduct a common foreign policy (including defence and security policy).

■ The Commission would be capped at 15 full members.

■ The Charter of Fundamental Rights to become legally binding.

■ The various Treaties on which the EC/EU is based would be fully consolidated into one document.

■ Existing Member States would be allowed to negotiate withdrawal from the EC/EU (no State has ever withdrawn).

The draft Constitution was signed by the heads of State of the 25 Member States in October 2004. The next stage in bringing the Constitution into effect was ratification, either by the EU's Member States' parliaments or their citizens in a referendum. All of the Member States were required to vote in favour. The ratification process had started in a relatively uncontroversial fashion. By the end of May 2005, the parliaments of eight countries (Austria, Germany, Greece, Hungary, Italy, Lithuania, Slovakia and Slovenia) had voted in favour. A successful referendum was held in Spain in February 2005 (with nearly 77 per cent voting yes).

However, the ratification process was thrown into turmoil and confusion when the French voted '*non*' in a referendum at the end of May 2005 (with nearly 55 per cent voting against the Constitution from a very high turnout, over 69 per cent of the electorate), followed a few days later by an even more emphatic '*nee*' in the Netherlands (nearly 62 per cent voting against).

The Constitutional Treaty was subsequently abandoned and an alternative Treaty was negotiated called the Treaty of Lisbon which was signed by heads of state on 13 December 2007. It is hoped that this will be ratified by Member States by the end of 2008 and come into force on 1 January 2009.

Unlike the failed Constitution, the Treaty of Lisbon does not replace the Treaties but instead amends the EC Treaty and the Treaty on European Union. The key proposals are as follows:

■ an elected president (elected by the European council by a qualified majority) for a term of two and a half years renewable once, thereby replacing the current six monthly rotating presidency, which is held by a Member State not by a person.

■ A new post of high representative of the EU for foreign affairs and security policy. It is believed that this will increase the impact, coherence and the visibility of the EU's external actions.

■ Reduction of the size of the European Commission from 1 November 2014 when it shall consist of a number of members corresponding to two thirds of the number of Member States (i.e. 18 instead of the present 27 Commissioners). They would be chosen on a rotation system between Member States. This will prevent the Commission becoming too large and unwieldy.

■ The Charter of Fundamental Rights 2000 would be part of the EU's primary law. (The UK has obtained a legally binding protocol providing that no court can rule that the laws, regulations or administrative provisions or practices of the UK are inconsistent with the principles laid down in the Charter of Fundamental Rights. Furthermore, that the Charter creates no new rights enforceable in the UK over and above those already existing in UK domestic law.

■ The EU shall have legal personality.

■ The Treaty provides that the Council shall act by qualified majority voting except where the Treaties provide otherwise. This means that qualified majority voting will become the normal voting system in the Council of the European Union.

■ The Treaty provides that any Member State may decide to withdraw from the Union in accordance with its own constitutional requirements.

■ The Treaty provides that the Union will get an extended capacity to act on freedom, security and justice.

■ The Treaty provides a strengthened role for the European Parliament by extending the co-decision procedure and placing the European Parliament on a more equal footing with the Council of the European Union.

GENERAL PRINCIPLES OF COMMUNITY LAW

In every legal system, the written sources of law do not provide the answer to every problem which appears before the courts. The ECJ has therefore had to develop general principles of law to provide a foundation for judgment.

SOURCES OF GENERAL PRINCIPLES

The Treaties also provide specific justification for the development of general principles of law.

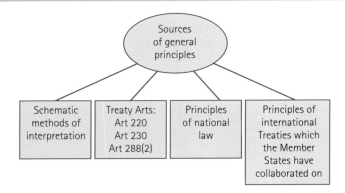

- *Article 220*: the ECJ shall ensure that in the interpretation and application of the Treaty the law is observed. Article 220 implies that 'the law' includes not only the written sources of law in the Treaty itself but also general principles created by the judiciary.
- *Article 230*: this lays down the grounds on which a Community act may be annulled. One of these grounds is 'infringement of this Treaty or any rule of law relating to its application'. The phrase 'any rule of law' must refer to something other than the Treaty itself.

- *Article 288(2)*: this is concerned with non-contractual liability and provides that the liability of the Community is based on 'the general principles common to the laws of the Member States'.

Principles of the national laws of the Member States
The ECJ has adopted principles taken from national laws of Member States. A principle need not be one of every Member State. Whatever the origin of the principle, it will be applied by the ECJ as a principle of Community law, not national law.

Principles of human rights in International Treaties
The ECJ, in the case of *Nold v Commission* [1974], held that the general principle of fundamental rights was also inspired by Treaties on which the Member States have collaborated or of which they are signatories.

FUNDAMENTAL HUMAN RIGHTS

Every Member State is a signatory of the European Convention on Human Rights. The commitment of the Union to human rights is enshrined in Art 6 TEU. This constituted a recognition of the long standing practice of acceptance of fundamental human rights as a general principle of Community law, which started with the case of *Stauder v City of Ulm* [1969].

The rights which have been recognised by the ECJ include:

- property rights, although these are not absolute and unqualified (*Nold v Commission* [1974]);

- religious rights (*Prais v Council* [1976]);

- right to privacy (*National Panasonic (UK) Ltd v Commission* [1979]), although this did not extend to the issue of seizing goods for the purposes of EC competition law;

- right to client–lawyer privacy (*AM and S Europe v Commission* [1982]);

- due process of law (*Musique Diffusion Francaise SA v Commission* [1984]);

- non-retroactivity of criminal law (*R v Kirk* [1984]);

- principle of legal review (*Heylens* [1987]).

PRINCIPLE OF EQUALITY

The EC Treaty contains specific examples of the principle of equality, as follows:

- discrimination on grounds of sex, nationality, racial or ethnic origin, religion or belief, disability, age or sexual orientation are prohibited (Arts 12 and 13);

- discrimination between producers and employers in agricultural production is prohibited (Art 34);

- discrimination between employees on grounds of sex is prohibited (Art 141).

The ECJ has taken these specific examples and deduced from them a general principle of equality (*Frilli* [1972]).

The principle of equality means that persons in similar situations are not to be treated differently, unless the difference in treatment is objectively justified.

PROPORTIONALITY

This is a principle borrowed from German law. According to this principle, a public authority may not impose obligations on a citizen except to the extent that they are strictly necessary for or proportionate to the aim that is sought.

LEGAL CERTAINTY

Legal certainty is a part of most legal systems, but in Community law the concept has become more complex, with various sub-concepts such as non-retroactivity, vested rights and legitimate expectations. (*Kolpinghuis Nijmegen* [1986]).

Non retroactivity and 'vested rights'

The concept of vested rights is often no more than another aspect of retro-activity, but it can also refer to such matters as the rule of law and the independence of the judiciary. They are rights acquired within the society's legal framework and under due process. The idea is that, at any given time, a person should know his legal position, and rights should not be taken away by retrospective legislation.

There are two rules relating to non-retroactivity. First, legislation is interpreted with a presumption that it is intended not to have retrospective effect. Secondly, although there is a general rule which prevents retroactivity, it is allowed where the purpose of a measure would be defeated, provided legitimate expectations are respected.

Legitimate expectations

This is another concept which has been borrowed from German law. It was first applied in *Commission v Council* (*First Staff Salaries* case) [1973]. The Council had agreed a pay formula for Commission staff which was to last for three years. Before the three years had expired, the Council attempted to impose a new formula. It was held that the new pay scales were invalid as they infringed legitimate expectations.

LEGAL PROFESSIONAL PRIVILEGE

It was recognised in *AM and S v Commission* [1979] that confidentiality of written communications between lawyer and client was a general principle of

Community law, but it was subject to two conditions. First, the communication must be for the client's defence. Secondly, the lawyer must be in private practice.

It was held in *National Panasonic (UK) Ltd v Commission* [1979] that, where a party was attempting to use legal professional privilege to thwart the enforcement of Community competition law, there was no violation of a right to privacy.

DUE PROCESS AND NATURAL JUSTICE

This principle has been drawn from English law and requires the making and enforcement of rules of conduct to comply with due process. For example, it was held in *Transocean Paint Association v Commission* [1974] that, where a person's interests are affected by a decision of a public authority, that person must be given the opportunity to make his view known before the decision is heard.

SECONDARY LEGISLATION

The EC Treaty defines three types of legally binding acts:

1 regulations;
2 directives;
3 decisions.

It also includes two non-legally binding acts:

1 recommendations;
2 opinions.

REGULATIONS

Article 249 provides that regulations have general application. They are also binding in their entirety and are directly applicable in all Member States. As to the meaning of 'direct applicability', see Chapter 2. Regulations help to ensure uniformity of law throughout the EC. They are normative in character and will apply generally or to groups of people identifiable in the abstract.

DIRECTIVES

Article 249 provides that directives are binding 'as to the result to be achieved'. They are binding on the Member States and do not bind individuals until they have been transposed into national law. Although they are binding on the Member States, the choice of form and methods when transposing them into national law is left to the national authorities. The purpose of directives is to set a common aim for the Member States. The Member States can then use the most appropriate methods for achieving this aim in their own legal system.

It has been held by the ECJ that directives may have direct effect. This is discussed in Chapter 2.

Individuals may be able to apply for compensation when they have suffered loss as a result of the incorrect transposition of a directive. This is discussed in Chapter 2.

	Regulations	Directives
Bind	People generally	Member States
Extent to which they bind	In their entirety	Result to be achieved
Need national measures?	No	Must have implementary measures

DECISIONS

Article 249 provides that decisions are binding on those to whom they are addressed. They can be addressed to individual Member States, corporations or private individuals. They differ from regulations, in that they personally address people as opposed to applying to people or groups of people in the abstract.

RECOMMENDATIONS AND OPINIONS

Recommendations and opinions have no binding force and are of persuasive authority only. In *Grimaldi v Fonds des Maladies Professionnelles* [1988], the ECJ said that national courts are 'bound to take recommendations into consideration in deciding disputes submitted to them, in particular where they clarify the interpretation of national provisions adopted in order to implement them or where they are designed to supplement binding EEC measures'.

Problems with classification of legal acts

It was held in *Confederation Nationale des Producteurs de Fruits et Legumes v Council* [1962] that the legal classification of a legislative act will depend on its substance rather than its form. An act can be called a regulation, but if it is in substance a decision, it will be treated as such. Consequently, in *International Fruit Co NV v Commission (No 1)* [1970], what was termed a 'regulation' was, in fact, a bundle of decisions.

Article 249 envisages distinct roles for each of the different types of legislative acts. In practice, however, there has been a blurring of the different acts. The ECJ has ruled that directives and decisions may have direct effect, which makes them less distinct from regulations than one would suppose from a casual reading of Art 249. Directives have often been very detailed when their function was to set an aim which would be fulfilled through national implementing legislation. If the directive is highly detailed, then the Member State is not left with much discretion to frame the legislation in the most appropriate way to its own legal order.

It has been found that some legislative acts are 'hybrids' and are in part a regulation and in part a decision: *NTN Toyo Bearing Co Ltd v Council* [1979], *per* AG Warner.

The list of acts contained in Art 249 is not exhaustive. The ECJ has held that other types of act are legally binding. For example, in *Les Verts v European Parliament* [1986], a decision of the Bureau of the European Parliament relating to the distribution of funds prior to the 1984 direct elections was held to be a legally binding act.

AGREEMENTS WITH THIRD COUNTRIES

The ECJ applies agreements with third countries as an integral part of Community law. There are three types:

1   agreements between the Community and one or more third countries;
2   'mixed' agreements between the Community and Member States and the Community and third countries;
3   agreements between Member States and third countries which are only part of Community law in exceptional circumstances.

DECISIONS OF THE ECJ AND CFI

Case law of the ECJ and CFI is an important source of Community law. The Treaties and secondary legislation cannot cater for all situations or social and economic developments, and much of the work of the ECJ and CFI has been to fill the gaps in the law, and to interpret the Treaties and secondary legislation in accordance with the general objectives of the Treaties.

Some of the most important principles of Community law have been developed by the ECJ, e.g. the principle of direct effect, the principle of indirect effect, state liability for breach of Community law, and the principle of supremacy of Community law.

You should now be confident that you would be able to tick all of the boxes on the checklist at the beginning of this chapter. To check your knowledge of Sources of law why not visit the companion website and take the Multiple Choice Question test. Check your understanding of the terms and vocabulary used in this chapter with the flashcard glossary.

2

EC law and national law

Appreciate the difference between direct applicability and direct effect ☐

Understand when a Treaty article, regulation and decision have direct effect ☐

Understand when a directive has direct effect and be able to apply the criteria to a problem question ☐

Know what is meant by the principle of indirect effect and recognise its limitations ☐

Understand the criteria for the application of the Francovich principle ☐

Realise that the principle of effectiveness demands that national remedies and national procedural rules cannot make the exercise of Community law rights difficult or impossible to pursue and that the principle of equivalence requires that Community law actions cannot be treated less favourably than comparable actions derived from domestic law ☐

Understand how the ECJ has developed the principle of supremacy of Community law ☐

DIRECT EFFECT

DIRECT EFFECT OF TREATY PROVISIONS

Usually, international Treaties are agreements between governments and do not create rights for citizens enforceable before national courts.

The Community legal order differs from international law in this respect, as it does create rights for citizens which are enforceable before national courts. This is what is meant by direct effect.

The concept started with the case of *Van Gend en Loos v Nederlandse Administratie der Belastingen* [1963]. A private firm sought to invoke Community law against Dutch customs authorities in proceedings before a Dutch tribunal. A preliminary reference was made to the European Court of Justice (ECJ). The Dutch Government argued that an infringement of the Treaty did not give an individual the right to bring an action. Actions could only be brought against the government of a Member State by the Commission.

It was held that the Treaty created a 'new legal order' and created rights for individuals which became part of their legal heritage.

Directly effective EC law is that which gives rise to rights or obligations which individuals may enforce before their national courts.

Van Gend en Loos was brought on the basis of Art 25 (formerly Art 12), which is a negative obligation as it requires that Member States shall refrain from introducing any new customs duties on imports and exports.

The concept was extended in the case of *Alfons Lütticke GmbH v Commission* [1966], where it was held that a positive obligation could have direct effect once the time limit for implementation has expired.

The criteria for a provision to have direct effect were set out by AG Mayras, in *Reyners v Belgium* [1974], as follows:

- the provision must be clear and unambiguous;

- it must be unconditional;

- its operation must not be dependent on further action being taken by the Community or national authorities.

It can be deduced from this that certain provisions of the Treaty are not directly effective as they are too vague. Neither must there be any discretion attached to the implementation of the provision, nor must the right be dependent on some legislative or executive action of the Commission or a Member State, until such action has been taken or the time limit for taking action has expired.

Van Gend en Loos is an example of what is known as vertical direct effect. The obligation rested on an organ of the State and there was a corresponding right on individuals. It was held in *Defrenne v SABENA (No 2)* [1976] that Treaty obligations could be imposed on individuals as well as Member States, and this is called horizontal direct effect. The applicant was an air stewardess employed by SABENA. She brought an action against them based on Art 141 (formerly Art 119) which provides that men and women shall receive equal pay for equal work. The applicant claimed that male air stewards were paid more for performing exactly the same tasks as stewardesses and this was a breach of Art 141. SABENA had argued that the Treaty obligations could not be imposed on private persons as well as the State. The ECJ disagreed.

> ### ▶ DEFRENNE v SABENA (No 2) (Case 43/75)
>
> **An airline stewardess claiming equal pay as a male cabin steward relied on Art. 141 of the EC Treaty.**
>
> The ECJ ruled that a Treaty article has both vertical and horizontal direct effect provided that it is sufficiently precise and unconditional, i.e. it gave rights which could be enforced in a national court.

Other Treaty Articles capable of imposing obligations on individuals are Art 39 (formerly Art 48), which provides for the free movement of workers (*Angonese* [2000]) and Arts 81 and 82 (formerly Arts 85 and 86), which deal with competition law (*Courage Ltd v Crehan* [2001]).

Vertical direct effect

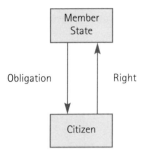

Horizontal direct effect

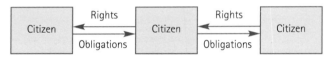

In addition to direct effect, there is a principle of 'direct applicability', which means that a provision becomes operative in a Member State immediately, without the need for the national legislature to pass implementing legislation to incorporate it into national law.

The terms 'direct applicability' and 'direct effect' have been used interchangeably by the ECJ, yet they are separate concepts. A provision can be directly applicable in the sense that it forms part of the law of a Member State in the absence of implementing legislation and yet not be sufficiently precise to have direct effect.

Conversely, a Community provision can be sufficiently precise to be relied on before a national court even though it has not been transposed into national law.

DIRECT APPLICABILITY OF REGULATIONS

Article 249 states that 'a regulation shall have general application. It shall be binding in its entirety and directly applicable in all Member States'.

As regulations are directly applicable, they do not need national implementing legislation. The ECJ went further in *Leonesio* [1972], where it said that not only is national implementing legislation unnecessary, it is illegal.

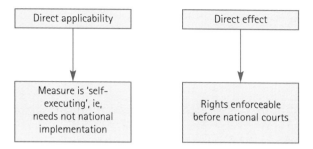

The ECJ felt that there would be three main dangers if regulations were to be implemented into national law:

1 it would be unclear whether they took effect from the date of the national measure or the date of the Community measure;

2 there would be subtle changes made to a regulation when transferred to national legislation;

3 it could prejudice the ECJ's jurisdiction to give a ruling on the interpretation and validity of the measure for the procedure for a preliminary reference.

Nevertheless, there are exceptions to the rule that regulations do not need national implementing legislation:

■ where the regulation expressly requires national implementing legislation: *Commission v United Kingdom* (*Tachograph* case) [1979];

■ where a regulation impliedly requires that a Member State brings forward national legislation, for example where the terms of a regulation are vague, though the national legislation must not be incompatible with the regulation;

■ a third possible area suggested by Hartley is where a Member State wishes to codify the law in a particular area, that is, draw all the relevant law on one particular topic into one piece of legislation.

DIRECT EFFECT OF DIRECTIVES

Article 249 states that directives are 'binding as to the result to be achieved' but that the choice of 'form and methods' is left to the Member State.

In contrast to regulations, the Treaty does not make any reference to directives being directly applicable. They cannot be directly applicable as they require national implementing legislation to give effect to them.

Despite the Treaty being silent on the point, the ECJ found that directives could have direct effect in *Van Duyn v Home Office* [1974].

▶ VAN DUYN v HOME OFFICE (Case 41/74)

The ECJ held that Directive 64/221 (which provided that measures taken on grounds of public policy or public security shall be based exclusively on the personal conduct of the individual) was sufficiently precise to have direct effect.

The main reasons why the ECJ gave direct effect to directives were:

- to make them more effective;
- to estop a Member State from relying on its own wrongdoing.

There was a strong reaction against giving direct effect to directives in the Member States, and the French Conseil d'État and initially the German Federal Tax Court denied that directives had direct effect.

The ECJ took this reaction into account, and in addition to having to satisfy the criteria for direct effect, the ECJ has placed two other important limitations on the direct effect of directives:

1 they cannot have direct effect before the time limit for implementation has expired: *Ratti* [1979];
2 they do not have horizontal direct effect: *Marshall v Southampton and South West Hampshire AHA (No 1)* [1986].

▶ PUBBLICO MINISTERO v RATTI (Case 148/78)

In his defence against a prosecution brought by the Italian state, Mr. Ratti sought to rely on an unimplemented directive.

The ECJ ruled that a directive has direct effect if it is clear and unconditional, the time for implementation has passed and the other party to the proceedings is the state.

A directive can be directly effective, and may be invoked as such, even though it has been transposed into national law: *VNO v Inspecteur der Invoerrechten en Accijnzen* [1977]; *Marks and Spencer* [2002].

The disadvantages of giving only vertical direct effect to directives have been identified as follows:

■ the effectiveness of directives within the national legal system is restricted;

■ the uniform application of Community law is restricted;

■ there is discrimination between individuals. For example, in employment law, a State employee can rely on a directive as against an employer, whereas a private employee cannot.

As a result of these difficulties, the ECJ has had to develop various strategies to circumvent the problems created by this limitation of the direct effect of directives (see below). One of these strategies has been to widen the definition of the State to enable as many people as possible to rely on directives – see emanation of the state (below).

It was confirmed in the cases of *Faccini Dori* [1994], *El Corte Inglés* [1996] and *Unilever* [2000] that directives do not have horizontal direct effect, but the ECJ suggested that an individual has other options for enforcing their rights either through indirect effect or under the *Francovich* principle. (See below.)

Directives can, however, have adverse legal consequences for individuals. In *CIA Security International SA v Signalson SA and Securitel SPRL* [1996], the claimant had brought proceedings against the two defendants in the Belgian courts, alleging unfair trading practices. The defendants claimed that the alarm system which was marketed by the claimant had not been approved as required by Belgian law. The claimant alleged that it was libelled by the defendants' claims and argued that it had not sought approval because the Belgian legislation breached EC law and, in particular, Directive 83/189, which required that the Member State notify the Commission about the technical standards of the alarms. It was held that the Belgian law had breached EC law and was therefore inapplicable to individuals. Consequently, the directive had adverse consequences for the defendants in their libel case.

Organ of the State/Emanation of the State

In *Marshall (No 1)*, the UK argued that where the State was acting as an employer, its position was no different from that of a private employer. The ECJ rejected this argument and held that it did not matter what capacity the State was acting in; directives could still be relied upon against it.

> ▶ **MARSHALL v SOUTHAMPTON & SOUTH WEST HAMPSHIRE AREA HEALTH AUTHORITY (Case 152/84)**
>
> The applicant sought to rely on the Equal Treatment directive against her employer. As her employer was a Health Authority, and thus an organ or the state, she could rely on the directive.

In *Foster v British Gas plc* [1990], the ECJ defined an 'organ of the State' as one that was offering a public service under the control of a public authority and which enjoyed special powers. The House of Lords, applying this test, held that British Gas (prior to privatisation) was an 'organ of the State'. There was some doubt as to whether the three criteria in *Foster* were alternatives or cumulative. It appears from *Rieser Internationale Transporte* [2004] that the criteria are cumulative, i.e. that a body is an emanation of the state if it provides a public service under state supervision and has for that purpose special powers.

> ▶ **FOSTER v BRITISH GAS PLC (Case C-188/89)**
>
> Mrs Foster sought to rely on the Equal Treatment directive in order to remain in work after the age of 60. The question arose as to whether British Gas was a state entity.

> The ECJ ruled that a state entity provides a public service under the control of the state and has special powers.

In *Johnston v Chief Constable of the Royal Ulster Constabulary* [1986], it was held that a directive could be relied on against a chief constable, as he is responsible for the direction of the police service. Since a police authority is charged by the State with the maintenance of public order and safety, it does not act as a private individual. On that basis, it could be regarded as an 'organ of the State'.

In *Jiménez Melgar* [2001], the claimant sought to rely upon Directive 92/85 against the Municipality of Los Barrios in southern Spain. The ECJ stated that 'It is settled case-law that the Member States' obligation arising from a directive to achieve the result prescribed by the directive ... is binding on all the authorities of the Member States, including decentralised authorities such as municipalities'.

In *Doughty v Rolls-Royce plc* [1992], the English Court of Appeal held that Rolls Royce (a nationalised body at the time which was the engine manufacturer for the Royal Air Force) was not an emanation of the state. Although the company was under the control of the state, the 'public service' was provided to the state, not to the public, nor did the company enjoy special powers of the type enjoyed by British Gas in *Foster*.

In *Griffin v South-West Water Services Ltd* [1995], the High Court held when applying the three *Foster* criteria, that South-West Water was an emanation of the state, despite being privatised. The judge made it clear that the question was not whether the body in question was under the control of the state, but whether the public service in question was under the control of the state.

DIRECT EFFECT OF DECISIONS

Under Art 249, a decision of the Council or Commission is binding on those to whom it is addressed. It can be addressed to Member States, individuals or corporations.

Decisions were held to be directly effective in *Grad v Finanzamt Traunstein* [1970]. Again, before they can be directly effective, they must fulfil the criteria for direct effectiveness.

DIRECT EFFECT OF INTERNATIONAL AGREEMENTS

Agreements with non-Member States have been held to be directly effective, even if they are not directly effective in the non-Member State: *Kupferberg* [1982].

DIRECT EFFECT – SUMMARY

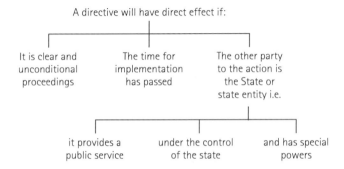

A directive will have direct effect if:

| It is clear and unconditional proceedings | The time for implementation has passed | The other party to the action is the State or state entity i.e. |

| it provides a public service | under the control of the state | and has special powers |

INTERPRETIVE OBLIGATION (INDIRECT EFFECT)

The main limitations on the direct effect of directives are that they cannot have horizontal direct effect, nor can they have direct effect before the time limit for implementation has expired. These limitations have meant that the effectiveness of directives has been seriously undermined. The ECJ has created an interpretive obligation on the national courts when interpreting national legislation, which to some extent circumvents these restrictions indirectly.

The origins of the obligation lie in the case of *Von Colson and Kamman v Land Nordrhein-Westfalen* [1984]. A German prison refused to engage two female social workers who were better qualified than the men who were employed in their place.

The equal treatment principle contained in Directive 76/207 had been infringed, but the German legislation implementing the directive limited the right to compensation to a nominal sum. The directive had not specified the form of the sanction for infringement of the equal treatment principle, but it was intended to be an adequate remedy. As there was a discretion in the hands of the Member States as to how the sanction was to be implemented, the

INTERPRETIVE OBLIGATION (INDIRECT EFFECT)

provision did not fulfil the criteria for direct effect. On a preliminary reference, the ECJ used Art 5 (now Art 10) of the EC Treaty which places Member States under an obligation to fulfil their Treaty obligations.

The ECJ said that Art 5 was an obligation addressed to all national authorities, including national courts. National courts are therefore under an obligation to interpret national legislation in accordance with the aims and purposes of directives.

A limitation was placed on the obligation by the ECJ, as it said that it only existed 'so far as it was possible' for the national court to give the national legislation a Community interpretation. Another uncertainty created by the case was that it involved legislation which had been introduced to implement the directive and it was unclear whether the obligation extended to legislation which was not framed with the intention of implementing a directive.

▶ VON COLSON v LAND NORDHREHIN (Case 14/83)

Germany had wrongly implemented a directive on equal employment rights.

The ECJ ruled that Member States, including national courts, should take all appropriate measures to give effect to Community law under Art 10 of the EC Treaty. Thus national courts were required to interpret their national law in the light of the aims of the wrongly implemented directive.

The existence of the obligation was reiterated in *Kolpinghuis Nijmegen BV* [1987], which added that the obligation existed between the date that the directive was adopted and the date of the time limit for its implementation into national law. This raises problems with regard to the concepts of legitimate expectations and non-retroactivity. Individuals will have arranged their affairs on the basis of national legislation as it has been implemented, and will not have bargained for a reinterpretation which effectively changes the law. In *Kolpinghuis Nijmegen BV* [1987], the ECJ stated that the interpretive obligation was subject to the general principles of legal certainty and non-retroactivity.

The guidelines for the interpretive obligation were extended in the case of *Marleasing SA v La Commercial Internacional de Alimentacion SA* [1992]. The claimant, Marleasing, sought to set aside the memorandum and articles of association of La Commercial on the grounds that, in the view of the claimant, it had been set up to put certain assets beyond the reach of creditors. The First Company Directive 68/55 exhaustively sets out the grounds on which a company can be declared void, and does not list fraud. However, the directive had not been transposed into Spanish law. The Spanish Civil Code was enacted before the directive and so could not possibly have been brought forward with the intention of implementing the legislation. Nevertheless, the ECJ said that the obligation extended to the Civil Code even though it had been enacted prior to the directive.

> ▶ MARLEASING SA v LA COMERCIAL INTERNACIONAL DE
> ALIMENTACION SA (Case C-106/89)
>
> **A directive which had not been implemented in Spain conflicted with the Spanish Civil Code.**
>
> The ECJ ruled that pre-dated or post-dated national legislation should be interpreted in the light of the aims of an unimplemented directive.

The obligation only exists where there are quite genuinely two possible ways in which to interpret the national legislation, one which accords with the directive and one which does not. In that situation, there is an obligation on the national court to give a Community interpretation. This was confirmed in the case of *Wagner Miret* [1995].

Further restrictions on the principle of indirect effect were laid down in *Arcaro* [1996]. The defendant appeared in criminal proceedings. There were doubts as to whether the Italian legislation conformed with two directives. The ECJ held that there was no obligation on a national court to interpret national law in accordance with a directive if this would lead to the imposition on an individual of criminal liability.

STATE LIABILITY IN DAMAGES

LIABILITY FOR NON-IMPLEMENTATION OF A DIRECTIVE

In *Francovich and Bonifaci v Italy* [1991], the applicants had been employees in businesses which became insolvent, leaving substantial arrears of salary unpaid. The Italian government had failed to implement a directive which had obliged them to set up a compensation scheme to protect employees of insolvent employers. This breach had been proved in enforcement proceedings taken against Italy.

The provisions of the directive did not have direct effect. Nevertheless, the ECJ held that Art 5 (now Art 10) of the EC Treaty requires Member States to fulfil their EC obligations, that the effectiveness of EC law would be called into question and the protection of EC law rights would be weakened, if individuals could not obtain compensation when their rights were infringed. On this basis, it was said to be inherent in the scheme of the Treaty that individuals should receive compensation from a Member State when it had breached its EC obligations. This right is subject to three conditions:

1. the directive must confer rights on individuals;
2. the content of these rights must be identifiable by reference to the directive;
3. there must be a causal link between the breach of a State's obligation and the damage suffered by the persons affected.

> ### ▶ FRANCOVICH v ITALY (Case C-6/90)
>
> **In breach of EC law, Italy failed to set up a scheme to compensate workers on the insolvency of their employers and a claim was brought by Mr Francovich.**
>
> **The ECJ ruled that Italy was in breach of its obligations and was liable in principle to compensate Mr Francovich who had suffered loss as a result of that breach.**

The issue of State liability for non-implementation of a directive arose again in *Dillenkofer* [1996]. The German government had failed to implement a directive concerned with the protection of individuals who booked package holidays. As a result of this failure, the applicants had suffered financial loss when certain companies collapsed. The ECJ held that a failure to implement a directive is in itself a serious breach of Community law, which gives rise to a right to damages if the three conditions laid down in *Francovich* are satisfied.

The ECJ also rejected the argument that the State could only be liable depending on the circumstances that caused it to miss the deadline. A Member State may not rely on difficulties in its own internal legal system to justify its failure to observe the obligations and time limits laid down by a directive.

LIABILITY FOR BREACHES OTHER THAN NON-IMPLEMENTATION OF A DIRECTIVE

The decision in *Francovich* left open a number of questions, including whether the State was under a liability to compensate for breaches of a directly effective Treaty provision or whether the State was liable where it had implemented a directive but the implementation was subsequently discovered to be incorrect.

The joined cases of *Factortame (No 3)* and *Brasserie du Pêcheur* [1996] dealt with the question of State liability for breaches of a directly effective Treaty provision. In the first case, the applicants, a group of Spanish fishermen, claimed damages as a result of not being able to fish in British waters during the period of 1 April 1989 to 2 November 1989 when the Merchant Shipping Act 1988 had laid down certain restrictions relating to the nationality, domicile and residence of the owners and managers of fishing vessels and of shareholders and directors of vessel owning and managing companies. These restrictions were designed to discourage 'quota hopping' in the fishing industry and had been found to be in breach of Art 43 (formerly Art 52) of the EC Treaty in earlier enforcement proceedings. In *Brasserie du Pêcheur*, the claimant had been prevented from exporting French beer to Germany as a result of German beer purity laws. These laws prevented the use of certain ingredients in the brewing of beer and prohibited the use of additives in beer altogether. The German law had been held to be in breach of Art 28 (formerly Art 30) of the EC Treaty in earlier enforcement proceedings brought in 1987. The French brewers sued the German Government for compensation for the period that they had been unable to export beer to Germany.

The ECJ held that there could be liability for State breaches of directly effective Treaty provisions. This principle of State liability includes acts of the legislature which are in breach of Community law and is inherent in the scheme of the Treaty. The Court noted that in both cases the legislature had a wide discretion. In *Factortame*, its discretion concerned the registration of fishing vessels, whereas in *Brasserie du Pêcheur* its discretion covered the regulation of foodstuffs.

The discretion enjoyed by these legislatures was analogous to that of Community institutions when enacting Community legislation. In these circumstances, there would be liability where three conditions were satisfied:

1   the rule of law must be intended to confer rights on individuals;
2   the breach must be sufficiently serious;
3   there must be a direct causal link between the breach of the obligation and the damage suffered by the parties.

It is for a national court to determine whether these criteria have been satisfied. These principles have been developed by reference to Art 288 of the EC Treaty, which is the provision dealing with the liability of Community institutions. What is striking is that the fact that a Member State has breached Community law is not, in itself, sufficient to ensure compensation. The breach must be 'sufficiently serious'.

The ECJ provided some guidance as to what would constitute a sufficiently serious breach. The decisive test was whether the Member State had 'manifestly and gravely disregarded the limits on its discretion'. The factors which could be taken into account by a national court were:

- the clarity and precision of the rule breached;

- the measure of discretion left to national or Community authorities;

- whether the infringement and damage caused was intentional or voluntary;

- whether any error of law was excusable;

- the fact that a position taken by a Community institution might have contributed to the omission;

- the adoption or retention of measures contrary to Community law.

Any breach which persisted after a judgment in enforcement proceedings or where there had been a preliminary ruling or settled case law of the Court, so that it was clear that the conduct in question constituted an infringement, would be 'sufficiently serious'. The ECJ made it clear that discrimination on grounds of nationality, as in *Factortame (No 3)*, would be sufficiently serious.

▶ R v SECRETARY OF STATE FOR TRANSPORT EX PARTE FACTORTAME LTD (Case C–213/89)

This case involved the Merchant Shipping Act 1988 which was in breach of Art 52 of the EC Treaty which provides for the right of establishment.

In this case (joined with *Brasserie de Pêcheur* above), the ECJ redefined the conditions for state liability for breach of EC law.

See also *Brasserie du Pêcheur SA v Germany* below.

When *Brasserie du Pêcheur* returned to the German Federal Court, it had found that the incompatibility of the German beer purity laws with Art 28 was not conclusive before the Commission had successfully taken enforcement proceedings against Germany. In the opinion of the German court, the case law of the ECJ on the question of the use of additives was not conclusive before 1987. The German court went on to decide that the cause of the beer's ban from the German market was the use of additives. Consequently, there was no direct causal link between the breach of Art 28 by the German rule and the loss suffered by the claimants. They failed to receive any compensation.

▶ BRASSERIE DU PÊCHEUR SA v GERMANY (Case C46/93)

The case concerned a German beer purity law which breached Art 28 of the EC Treaty.

The ECJ ruled that a state incurs liability for breach of EC law if the rule of EC law confers rights on individuals, the breach is sufficiently serious and there is a causal link between the breach and the individual's loss.

See also *R v Secretary of State for Transport ex parte Factortame Ltd* above.

When the House of Lords gave judgment in *R v Secretary of State for Transport ex p Factortame (No 5)* [1999], it held that the British legislation was discriminatory on grounds of nationality, in breach of clear and unambiguous rules of EC law, and was sufficiently serious to give rise to a right to damages for individuals who had suffered loss. As a result, the UK Government faced a £100 million bill for compensation.

The case of *R v Minister of Agriculture, Fisheries and Food ex p Hedley Lomas* [1996] concerned the refusal of the UK Government to issue licences for the export of live animals to Spain as it felt that standards in slaughter houses there contravened a directive. Hedley Lomas, a company, had been refused an export licence and claimed that it was a breach of Art 34 (now Art 29) of the EC Treaty. The ECJ stated that the mere infringement of Community law might be 'sufficiently serious' where the Member State was not called upon to make any legislative choices and had reduced or no discretion. The UK had not even proved that the Spanish slaughter houses were falling below the standards laid down in the directive.

The question of an incorrect transposition of a directive was considered in *R v HM Treasury ex p British Telecommunications plc* [1996]. The ECJ held that the provision of the directive in question was imprecise and was reasonably capable of bearing the meaning ascribed to it by the UK Government. The interpretation had been shared by other Member States and was not contrary to the wording or objective of the directive. Despite having said previously that it is a matter for a national court to determine whether the criteria for liability have been satisfied, it said in this case that it was in possession of all the information and that the breach was not 'sufficiently serious'. Although the UK was in breach of Community law, this did not give the company affected a right to compensation, as the breach was not 'sufficiently serious'.

Other state liability claims based on incorrectly implemented directives include *Rechberger & Others v Austria* [1999] and *Stockholm Lindöpark v Sweden* [2001]. In both cases the claimants were successful. In *Rechberger* the claimants argued that Austria had imposed limitations on consumers' rights when implementing Art 7 of Directive 90/314. The ECJ agreed that there was no 'margin of discretion' as to the wording of the implementing legislation, the Austrian legislation was therefore 'manifestly incompatible' with the obligations under the directive and thus a sufficiently serious breach of Community law had occurred. In *Stockholm Lindöpark* the question was whether Sweden had correctly implemented the sixth VAT directive.

The Court held not, stating: 'Given the clear wording of the Sixth Directive, the Member State concerned was not in a position to make any legislative choices ...'

In *Haim v Kassenzahnärztliche Vereinigung Nordrhein* [2000] it was held that compensation for non-compliance with community law could be claimed with regard to the actions of a public body, as well as those of a Member State. Furthermore, it was held that the compensation could be claimed directly from the public body. The result is that a public body may be held financially accountable for non-compliance even if its actions were limited by national legislation.

Köbler

In *Köbler v Austria* [2003], the ECJ held that there was no reason why a *Francovich* claim could not be brought against a national supreme court. K, an Austrian national, had brought an unsuccessful challenge to a provision of Austrian legislation which he alleged contravened his rights under Art 39 (see Chapter 5). However, the Austrian Supreme Court rejected his claim. K then brought a *Francovich* action, asserting that the Austrian court had misapplied an earlier ECJ ruling, that this constituted a 'sufficiently serious breach' and that he was therefore entitled to compensation. The ECJ agreed that, in principle, K's claim was valid. The same conditions applied as in any *Francovich* claim, although it was said that 'liability can be incurred only in the exceptional case where the national court has manifestly infringed the applicable law and the Court's case-law in the matter'. Applying this point, the ECJ decided that, although the Austrian court had committed a breach of Community law, it was not sufficiently serious.

> ### ▶ KÖBLER v AUSTRIA (Case C–224/01)
>
> Mr Köbler brought an action for damages against an Austrian court for failure to apply Community law. He did not succeed because the breach of Community law by the Austrian court was not sufficiently serious.

Procedural remedies

In addition to the substantive right to damages, the ECJ has also ensured the effective protection of Community rights through the creation of effective procedural remedies.

In *R v Secretary of State ex p Factortame Ltd (No 1)* [1990], it was held by the ECJ that where a national court considered that the sole obstacle to granting interim relief was a rule of national law, it was obliged to set aside that rule. This ruling has been interpreted as creating a new procedural remedy for the protection of Community rights.

On reference back to the House of Lords from the ECJ in *R v Secretary of State ex p Factortame Ltd (No 2)* [1990], it was held that, in considering interim relief, the court has to consider, first, the availability to either claimant or defendant of an adequate remedy in damages and, secondly, if no such adequate remedy existed, the balance of convenience, taking all the circumstances into consideration.

Procedural rules were also considered in *Peterbroeck, van Campenhout & Cie SCS v Belgium* [1995]. The appellant company disputed the amount of tax it had to pay. Its claim was rejected by the Belgian tax authorities. It appealed to the Court of Appeal and for the first time claimed that the tax was contrary to EC law. Under Belgian law, a new plea could only be raised within a time limit of 60 days and this time had been exceeded. The Court of Appeal was the first body in the proceedings to have the jurisdiction to make a preliminary reference, and the issue could not have been considered at any other stage in the proceedings.

The ECJ held that Community law precludes a domestic procedural rule which prevents the national court from considering the compatibility of domestic law with Community law, unless it can be justified on the ground of legal certainty or the proper conduct of procedure.

The obligation to disapply national rules only applies where it would make the application of Community law impossible or excessively difficult. The facts differed in *van Schijndel and van Veen v Stichting Pensioenfonds voor Fysiotherapeuten* [1995]. The applicants had not made pension contributions to a compulsory pension scheme. Before the lower courts, the applicants had argued that they did not have to make such contributions under Dutch law. On their second appeal to the Supreme Court of the Netherlands, they argued that the pension was contrary to EC competition law and that, although they had not argued this point on their first appeal, the court should have applied EC law on its own motion. The Supreme Court of Appeal could consider new submissions only on points of law and not on points of fact. The first appeal court was not allowed to go beyond the issues raised by the parties themselves and, as the parties had not raised the issues relating to EC competition law, the court would not have applied the EC Treaty Articles itself.

It was held that Community law does not oblige national courts to abandon the passive role assigned to them by domestic procedural rules. Domestic law precluded the first appeal court from considering points which had not been raised by the parties, whether the claim related to domestic or to Community law. It therefore did not have to consider points not raised in order to protect Community law rights. Similarly, domestic law did not allow the Supreme Court of Appeal to consider points of fact in both domestic and Community cases. Therefore, it did not have to do so in this case, as the claimants were relying on facts which they had not relied on at first instance. In deciding whether the application of Community law was 'impossible or excessively difficult', the national rule had to be analysed by reference to its role in the procedure. In analysing domestic procedure, the protection of the rights of the defence, the principle of legal certainty and the proper conduct of procedure had to be taken into account.

Unlike in *Peterbroeck*, there had been an opportunity for a court to consider the compatibility of national law with Community law at first instance. The parties had failed to avail themselves of this opportunity and could not then rely on Community law to overturn domestic rules at a later stage in the proceedings. In some jurisdictions, courts are either obliged or have a discretion to consider legal grounds that have not been raised by the parties. Where this is the position under domestic law, the national courts must consider the Community rights even if the parties have failed to do so. This means that the application of Community law can differ form State to State.

In *Emmott v Minister for Social Welfare* [1991], it was held that, where a directive has not been correctly transposed into national law, time does not start to run for the purpose of limitation periods until the directive is properly implemented into national law. This is so even in respect of non-directly effective rights and also where the ECJ has not declared that the Member State has failed to fulfil its obligations. In other words, time does not start to run until an individual is certain of what his legal rights are.

The rule in *Emmott* was not applied in the case of *Steenhorst-Neerings* [1993]. This case involved a restriction on the applicant's right to claim welfare payments retrospectively which had been denied to her on discriminatory grounds. The ECJ held that there were material differences between this and the *Emmott* case. In *Steenhorst-Neerings*, the directive had been partially invoked and the restriction was implemented on grounds of legal certainty to prevent administrative claims stretching out indefinitely. That consideration did not apply in *Emmott* as the directive had not been correctly transposed and the rule could not be invoked at all. In *Steenhorst-Neerings*, the rule was designed to ensure good administration and the financial equilibrium of the Dutch welfare system.

Steenhorst-Neerings [1993] was followed in *Johnson v Chief Adjudication Officer (No 2)* [1994], despite certain important factual differences between the two cases. In *Johnson (No 2)*, retrospective claims to benefit which had been denied on discriminatory grounds were again restricted. However, it could not be argued that this had been done on grounds of good administration, as the burden of proof had been placed on the applicant. Nor could it be claimed that the rule had been imposed to protect the financial equilibrium of the scheme, as it was non-contributory.

Time limits also arose in the case of *Denkavit Internationaal BV v Kamer van Koophandel en Fabriken voor Midden-Gelderland* [1996]. The Netherlands Chambers of Trade and Industry imposed a levy on undertakings established within their areas. The question was whether it was compatible with a directive on capital duty, which prohibits the charging of taxes other than capital duty in respect of the registration of a capital company, or any other formality required before such a company commences business. There is a 30 day time limit laid down by national law for appeals against decisions in order to resist claims for the refund of fees charged in respect of earlier years. The ECJ held that the directive did not prohibit the levy and consequently felt that it did not need to consider the time limit. Advocate General Jacobs did consider the time limit and felt that the *Emmott* principle would be confined to exceptional circumstances. He did not feel that it was necessary to further qualify the *Emmott* principle by limiting it to a 'grave and manifest infringement of Community law', rejecting the possibility of a parallel between such cases and the conditions for State liability in damages.

In *Zuckerfabrik Süderdithmarschen AG v Hauptzollamt Itzehoe* [1991], it was held that the power of a national court to suspend administrative acts which are based on a Community measure whose validity is in doubt can only order a suspension on the same conditions as those applied by the ECJ in interim measure proceedings (under Arts 242 and 243 (formerly Arts 185 and 186)).

These conditions are as follows:

■ the national court must entertain serious doubts as to the validity of the Community act;

■ it must refer the question of validity to the ECJ (unless that question is already before the Court);

■ there must be a need for urgency and a threat of serious and irreparable damage to the applicant must exist;

■ the national court must take due account of the Community interest.

These conditions were again upheld in the case of *Atlanta v BEF* [1996]. The *Zuckerfabrik* [1991] case concerned a national court's power to suspend a national measure based on allegedly invalid Community legislation. In *Atlanta*, the ECJ held that an interim order could go beyond preserving the existing legal position of the parties and could be granted where it was intended to create a new legal position. In this latter respect, the national court is effectively suspending the application of the disputed act.

The ECJ went on to 'clarify' the *Zuckerfabrik* conditions. This clarification consisted of the following:

■ where the national court has 'serious doubts' as to validity, it must not only refer the question of validity to the ECJ but also set out the reasons why it is considered invalid;

■ the national court should bear in mind the discretion that the Community institutions must be allowed when implementing policy in the economic sector in question;

■ the national court must consider whether immediate enforcement of the act would result in irreversible damage (purely financial damage is not irreversible);

■ regulations must not be set aside without due consideration of the damage which the interim measure may cause to the legal regime established by that regulation for the Community as a whole;

■ if interim relief represents a financial risk to the Community, it may be necessary to require the applicant to provide adequate guarantees in the form of money or other security;

■ the national court must also take into account Art 230 judgments regarding the legislation in question.

PRIMACY OF EC LAW

TWIN PILLARS

The Community legal order is said to be built on the 'twin pillars' of direct effect and supremacy. The EC Treaty contains no express provision regarding the supremacy of EC law although there are inferences to that effect, e.g. Art 10.

It is the ECJ which has developed the principle of supremacy along with the first pillar of direct effect.

The case of *Van Gend en Loos v Nederlandse Administratie der Belastingen* [1963] first stated the principle of supremacy when it held that a Treaty provision took priority over a conflicting piece of earlier Dutch legislation. The case is better known for laying the other pillar of the legal order, namely, the principle of direct effect.

▶ VAN GEND EN LOOS (case 26/72)

The ECJ ruled that Art 25 of the EC Treaty requiring Member States to refrain from introducing new customs duties, was unconditional and gave rise to rights and obligations which could be enforced in national courts.

The second pillar of the supremacy of Community law was laid in the case of *Costa v ENEL* [1964]. The ECJ held that Community law could not be overridden by domestic legal provisions, regardless of whether the provisions came earlier or later than Community law.

The 'twin pillars' of European legal order

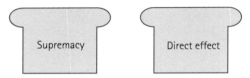

Supremacy

Direct effect

The basis of the principle of supremacy was found to arise from the words and spirit of the Treaty rather than in national constitutions. This can be seen from a famous *dictum* of the ECJ in *Costa v ENEL*:

> The transfer by the States from their domestic legal system to the Community legal system of rights and obligations arising under the Treaty carries with it the permanent limitation of their sovereign rights against which a subsequent unilateral act incompatible with the concept of the Community cannot prevail.

The court argued that a restriction of sovereign rights and the creation of a body of law applicable to individuals as well as Member States made it necessary for this new legal order to override inconsistent provisions of national law. Community law was also prepared to reach into national law and provide remedies where national law did not do so.

Community law overrules provisions of national constitutions

This rule is an unconditional rule and applies to every rule of domestic law, whatever its standing. Consequently, Community law cannot be tested in municipal courts for compliance with constitutions of Member States.

In *Internationale Handelsgesellschaft mbH v Einfuhr und Vorratsstelle für Getreide* [1970], it was held that recourse to the legal rules or concepts of national law in order to judge the validity of measures adopted by the Community would have an adverse effect on the uniformity and efficacy of Community law.

Therefore, the validity of a Community measure or its effect within a Member State cannot be affected by allegations that it runs counter to either fundamental rights as formulated by the constitution of that State or the principles of a national constitutional structure.

Principle of supremacy must be applied immediately

Supremacy is a rule which is addressed to the national courts and is to be applied immediately by every national court.

In *Administrazonie delle Finance dello Stato v Simmenthal SpA* [1978], an Italian court was faced with a conflict between a Council regulation and Italian laws, some of which were subsequent in time to the Italian regulation. Under Italian law, legislation contrary to EC regulations can be declared unconstitutional, but only by the constitutional court and not by ordinary courts. The Italian judge made a preliminary reference on the question of whether direct applicability of regulations required national courts to disregard inconsistent subsequent national legislation without waiting for relevant legislation to be enacted by the national legislature.

It was held that every national court must apply Community law in its entirety and must accordingly set aside any provision of national law which may conflict with it.

If national law impairs the effectiveness of Community law by withholding the power to set aside an inconsistent piece of national law, then that rule is contrary to Community law.

Member States cannot plead force majeure

A Member State cannot say that it has tried to comply with an obligation or remedy a breach but has been prevented by legislation from doing so.

In *Commission v Italy* (*First Art Treasures* case) [1968], an Italian tax on art treasures was in violation of Italy's obligation under Art 16 (now repealed) to abolish customs duties on exports. The ECJ held that, by continuing to levy the tax, Italy was in breach of Community law. Legislation had been introduced but lapsed with the dissolution of the Italian Parliament. The Government's inability to force the legislation through was not an excuse for failing to give effect to the principle of supremacy.

Supremacy applies regardless of source of law

The principle applies regardless of the *source* of national law. Both inconsistent statutes and judicial precedents have been declared inapplicable, and rules of professional bodies may also be held inconsistent and inapplicable: *R v Royal Pharmaceutical Society of Great Britain* [1989].

Supremacy applies regardless of form of Community law

The principle of supremacy applies to different forms of Community law. Consequently, it will apply whether the Community provision is a Treaty Article, a Community act or an agreement with a third country.

Member States must repeal conflicting legislation

Member States are obliged to repeal conflicting national legislation, even though it is merely 'inapplicable' and not enforced: *Commission v France* (*French Merchant Seamen* case) [1974].

A French law provided that a certain proportion of the crew on French merchant ships had to be of French nationality. This was in conflict with Community law, and enforcement proceedings were brought against France. The French Government argued that the law had not been applied and, as it was regarded as inapplicable, France had not violated the Treaty.

The ECJ held that the existence of the law created 'an ambiguous state of affairs' which would make seamen uncertain as to the possibilities available to them of relying on Community law. It was not enough simply not to enforce the law: it had to be repealed.

You should now be confident that you would be able to tick all of the boxes on the checklist at the beginning of this chapter. To check your knowledge of EC law and national law why not visit the companion website and take the Multiple Choice Question test. Check your understanding of the terms and vocabulary used in this chapter with the flashcard glossary.

3

Community institutions

Know the composition and functions of the three political institutions, i.e. the Commission, the Council of the European Union and the European Parliament ■

Appreciate the supervisory role of the European Parliament over the Commission and to a lesser extent the Council of the European Union ■

Be able to criticise the current institutional structure ■

Understand the role of the European Council ■

Be able to describe in outline the decision making process ■

Know the composition of the ECJ and CFI and their jurisdiction ■

Be aware of the procedure in the ECJ ■

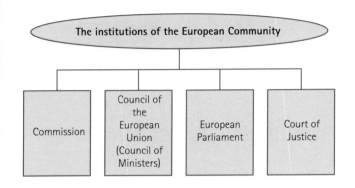

THE COMMISSION

FUNCTIONS

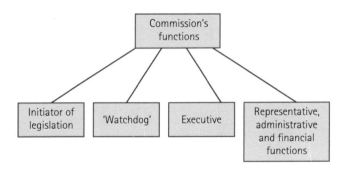

Initiator of Community action

The Commission has historically had the right of legislative initiative, and Council decisions are taken on the basis of Commission proposals. Under Art 192 (formerly Art 138b) of the EC Treaty, the European Parliament can 'request' a proposal when it considers legislation to be necessary. The Commission does not accept that it must bring forward legislative proposals when faced with such a request.

Under Art 208 (formerly Art 152) of the EC Treaty, the Council of the European Union may request that the Commission undertakes any study that the Council considers desirable for the attainment of common objectives and to submit to it any appropriate proposals.

Watchdog, i.e. Guardian of the Treaties

The Commission acts as the 'watchdog' of the European Community, either through enforcement proceedings or through its role in competition law.

Articles 226 and 227 of the EC Treaty: the Commission is in a unique position regarding enforcement proceedings. Under Art 226 and Art 227 proceedings, the Commission can take Member States which are in breach of their Treaty obligations before the European Court of Justice (ECJ). The procedure is in two stages. The first is an informal stage whereby the Commission issues a formal notice and eventually issues a reasoned opinion to the Member State which delimits the nature of the dispute. In practice, the Commission attempts to negotiate a settlement with the Member State, and the majority of cases are settled at the informal stage. The second stage is the formal litigation stage where the Commission takes the errant Member State before the ECJ.

Article 227 proceedings involve one Member State taking another Member State before the ECJ, but even with this procedure the Member State must first take its complaint before the Commission, which will issue a reasoned opinion. In practice, if there is substance to the complaint, then the Commission will take the complaint over. Consequently, Art 227 is rarely used.

As the Commission is involved in all enforcement proceedings and negotiates the outcome of most such proceedings, it is in a distinctive position. *Snyder* [1993] 56 MLR 19 argues that this enables the Commission to use litigation to develop long term strategies and establish basic principles. For example, in the years prior to the 1 January 1993 deadline for the European internal market, most enforcement proceedings related to the non-implementation of directives. Art 226 was being used as a tool to ensure the success of the internal market programme.

The Member State is required to comply with the declaratory judgment of the ECJ under Art 228(1). If the Member State fails to comply, then the Commission may take further action against the Member State under Art 228(2).

The procedure follows a similar pattern to that under Art 226 above. The Commission will provide the Member State with an opportunity to submit its observations on the alleged breach, following which the Commission will issue a reasoned opinion requiring the Member State to comply with the ECJ's judgment within a reasonable period of time. If the Member State does not comply with this reasoned opinion, then the Commission may once again refer the case to the ECJ.

However, this time, the ECJ has the power under Art 228(2) to impose a financial penalty (either a lump sum payment or a penalty payment) on the Member State for non-compliance with its judgment, e.g. in 1997, the ECJ imposed a penalty payment of 20,000 euros per day on Greece for each day of delay in complying with EC law regarding the disposal of toxic waste.

Competition law: in the past, the Commission had the central role in enforcing EC competition law (e.g. regarding anti-competitive agreements prohibited by Art 81 or abuse of a dominant position prohibited by Art 82).

Following enlargement in 2004, a new decentralised system came into place when Regulation 1/2003 came into force. This took the pressure off the Commission which is now assisted by national competition authorities (NCAs) when enforcing EC competition law. In the UK, the Office of Fair Trading is one of the NCAs.

The Commission may now focus its attention on the more serious breaches of Art 81 and Art 82. Both the Commission and NCAs have the power to impose fines on undertakings which are in breach of EC competition law, e.g. in 2004, the Commission imposed a fine of Euros 497 million on Microsoft.

Executive of the Community

The Commission is often called the Executive of the Community. The term is misleading and the Commission's role has fluctuated between a prototype federal government and a secretariat simply carrying out the instructions of the Council of Ministers. The change in role has been a response to historical circumstances. Unlike the Parliament, which has seen a steady increase in its powers since the Treaty of Rome, the Commission has seen peaks and troughs in its powers. The key dates are as follows:

1958–65: This period was the high point of the Commission's powers, when it seemed to be evolving into some sort of federal government. It negotiated the elimination of customs tariffs and a common agricultural policy, although it had less success with the establishment of a common external tariff, internal liberalising measures and energy and transport policy.

1966 – Luxembourg Accords: This convention was developed in response to a constitutional crisis in the Community. Where the vital interests of a Member State are at stake, it can veto a legislative proposal. The Community was put on a more inter-governmentalist footing and the Commission took on more of the characteristics of a secretariat.

The status of the Luxembourg Accords was subsequently raised by the Treaty of Amsterdam, from that of a constitutional convention to being enshrined in the Treaty itself. The ECJ will now be able to rule on what constitutes a matter within a Member State's 'vital national interest'.

1974 – Formation of the European Council: This again gave a more inter-governmentalist flavour to the Community.

1986 – Single European Act (SEA): The 1992 deadline enhanced the Commission's role. It became more active in the legislative sphere and in negotiation with national governments.

1992 – Treaty on European Union: The Commission was on the wane again. The right of legislative initiative was diluted. The new legislative procedure in Art 189b (now Art 251) only allows for the Commission to mediate in the Conciliation Committee and its proposals can be amended by a qualified majority. This weakens the Commission, as it makes its proposals easier to change.

1997 – Treaty of Amsterdam: The ToA introduced amendments to the co-decision procedure laid down in Art 251 of the EC Treaty which further strengthened the hand of the European Parliament. The Commission is still left with a mediating role in the Conciliation Committee.

However, the European Parliament failed to secure a shared right of legislative initiative with the Commission. The European Parliament had requested at the Inter-Governmental Conference (IGC) which preceded the ToA that the Commission be forced to respond to its requests for legislative proposals, but such a right was not granted.

The Commission has a small, primary legislative power. In *France, Italy and United Kingdom v Commission* [1980], it was held that the Commission had a right to legislate where it is clear from a purposive interpretation of a Treaty provision that it was intended to give such a right to the Commission, e.g. under Art 86(3).

The Commission is often involved in the detailed implementation of Council decisions. This frequently involves further legislation and the Commission has been given wide powers of delegated legislation. The Council has not relinquished total control over the delegated legislation and retains varying degrees of control.

Recommendations and opinions
The Commission can formulate recommendations or opinions on matters dealt with in the Treaty.

Representative, financial and administrative functions
The Commission has a number of representative, financial and administrative functions:

- it represents the Member States in negotiations with non-Member States;

- it is responsible for the administration of Community funds.

COMPOSITION
Prior to the EU's enlargement in May 2004, there were 20 members of the Commission, appointed by the governments of the Member States. The five biggest states (France, Germany, Italy, Spain and the UK) had two Commissioners and the other States one each. However, the enlargement into central and eastern Europe meant that maintaining this system would have left the Commission unmanageably large and so, from November 2004, the rules were

changed so that every Member State had one Commissioner regardless of population size or economic strength (in other words, Germany has one Commissioner as does Malta). Thus, there are now a total of 27 Commissioners.

The powers of the European Parliament over the appointment of European Commissioners has been extended by both the TEU and the ToA. Currently, under Art 214(2), the governments of the Member States nominate by common accord the person they wish to be President of the European Commission.

This nomination is subject to the approval of the European Parliament. The governments of the Member States then, by common accord with the nominee for President, nominate the people they wish to see serve as Commissioners. All nominees are then subject to a vote of approval by the European Parliament, after which they are appointed by common accord of the Member State governments.

Despite the careful attention to the representation of each Member State, Commissioners are not the representatives of national governments, and are required to act in the interests of the Union as a whole. They are required to be above national loyalties.

The Commission is headed by a President and there can be one or two Vice Presidents. The President of the Commission is its leader and most prominent member. This is recognised in Art 219, which states that the 'Commission shall work under the guidance of the President'.

The Commission is divided into departments called Directorates-General of which there are approximately 40. These Directorates-General are responsible for different aspects of Community policy and are clearly named, e.g. DG – Competition. Commissioners are given responsibility for particular DGs as part of their portfolio. Each DG is headed by a Director General who is responsible to the relevant Commissioner.

Directorates General are sub-divided into Directorates (headed by a Director), and these in turn are made up of Divisions (each under a Head of Division).

Each Commissioner is assisted by his Cabinet, which is a type of private office and consists of a group of officials appointed by him and directly responsible to him. The head of the Cabinet is known as the Chef de Cabinet. The Chefs de Cabinet meet regularly to co-ordinate activities and prepare the ground for Commission meetings. If the Chefs de Cabinet reach unanimous agreement on a question, then their decision is normally adopted by the Commission without debate.

Commissioners are appointed for five year renewable terms. All the terms expire together, so the whole of the Commission is reappointed at the same time. National governments cannot dismiss a Commissioner during a term of office; they can only fail to renew a term.

The Commission can be forced to resign *en bloc* by the Parliament, but this cannot be used to dismiss individual Commissioners.

The ECJ can compel a Commissioner to retire on grounds of serious misconduct or because he no longer fulfils the conditions required for the performance of his duties.

COUNCIL OF THE EUROPEAN UNION
(formerly the Council of Ministers)

The purpose of the Council of the European Union is to represent the national interest.

FUNCTIONS

Its functions are to:

- take general policy decisions;

- ensure that objectives set out in the Treaty are attained (Art 202);

- ensure co-ordination of general economic policies of Member States (Art 202);

- take decisions (generally based on Commission proposals);

- conclude agreements with foreign countries;

- jointly decide the budget with Parliament.

COMPOSITION

The Council is not a fixed body and each Member State is represented by a government minister. Which government minister attends the meeting will depend on the subject matter of the meeting. There are nine different types of Council meeting or 'configurations' as they are called, e.g. General Affairs and External Relations, Economic and Financial Affairs being two examples. The Member States will be represented by the government minister responsible for that particular specialisation.

PRESIDENCY

The Presidency of the Council rotates amongst the members at six-monthly intervals. While it holds the Presidency, a Member State will provide a President (chair) for all meetings of the Council. The President will call meetings, preside at them, call for a vote and sign acts adopted at the meeting. The Presidency also has responsibility to ensure the smooth running of the Council, will act as mediator between the Member States when searching for an agreement, and is the Union's representative to the outside world.

To a large extent, the Presidency will enable a Member State to control the agenda of the European Union, so a Member State will attempt to use the time that it holds the Presidency to push through as many measures as possible.

COREPER

The government ministers who comprise the Council of the European Union will have full time ministerial responsibilities in their own country, and as a result are only present in Brussels for short periods.

In order to provide continuity, a Committee of Permanent Representatives, known as COREPER, was established.

Each Member State has an ambassador to the Union, and these ambassadors are given the title 'Permanent Representatives'. Their function is to represent the Member States at a lower level than the Ministers.

In fact, there are two tiers to COREPER itself. Important political questions are dealt with by the Permanent Representatives themselves, and this is known as COREPER II.

More technical questions will be dealt with by deputy Permanent Representatives meeting known as COREPER I.

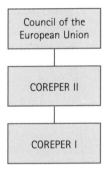

At a lower level still, COREPER is involved in the work of a plethora of sub-committees and working groups which examine Commission proposals. In these meetings, a Member State is often represented by a national expert.

COREPER has been called a 'mixed' institution, part of a 'grey zone' of institutions which cannot be classified as belonging either to the Union or to Member States.

VOTING

Article 205 provides: 'Save as otherwise provided in this Treaty, the Council shall act by a majority of its members.'

In practice, only a few unimportant matters are decided by a simple majority. Some matters, for example admission of new members, are decided unanimously. Most matters are decided by a 'qualified majority', where the votes of larger States have greater weight than the votes of smaller ones. Under Art 205, the votes of the Member States are weighted as follows:

France, Germany, Italy, UK	29 votes (each)
Spain, Poland	27 votes (each)
Romania	14 votes
Netherlands	13 votes
Belgium, Czech Republic, Greece, Hungary, Portugal	12 votes (each)
Austria, Sweden, Bulgaria	10 votes (each)
Denmark, Finland, Ireland, Lithuania, Slovakia	7 votes (each)
Cyprus, Estonia, Latvia, Luxembourg, Slovenia	4 votes (each)
Malta	3 votes
Total	345 votes

A qualified majority is 255 votes (representing 73.91 of the total votes). In other words, 91 votes will be needed to block a proposal.

'Double Majority'

In November 2004, a new procedure was introduced whereby, for a proposal to be adopted, a majority of Member States (ie at least 14 out of 27, regardless of size or population) must vote in favour. This is known as 'double majority'.

'Demographic safety net'

Another new rule introduced in November 2004 is the 'demographic safety net'. This means that each Member State can request verification of whether the qualified majority represents at least 62 per cent of the population of the EU. If this condition is not fulfilled, the decision cannot be adopted.

EUROPEAN COUNCIL

In 1974, it was agreed that the heads of government of the Member States, together with their foreign ministers, would hold summit conferences at regular intervals. These became known as the 'European Council' and achieved legal status by virtue of Art 2 of the SEA. The President of the Commission has been given the right to attend meetings.

The title 'European Council' is confusing, since it is not the same body as the Council of the European Union, though it can act as a Council of the European Union as there is nothing to prevent Member States being represented by their Heads of State or government.

The European Council possesses no formal powers. It is an informal forum for discussions relating to issues of common Community concern and is a vehicle for co-ordinating the Member States' foreign policies to ensure that they maximise their influence on world affairs. To this end, the SEA places an obligation 'to endeavour jointly to formulate and implement a European foreign policy'.

Article 4 of the TEU provides a further role for the European Council when it states that it shall 'provide the Union with the necessary impetus for its development and shall define the general political guidelines thereof'. The European Council is the focus of the inter-governmentalist activities under the Common Foreign and Security and Police and Judicial Co-operation in Criminal Matters pillars of the European Union.

The Presidency of the European Council is held by the Member State holding the Presidency of the Council of the European Union.

EUROPEAN PARLIAMENT

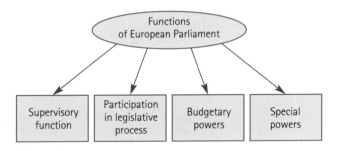

Purpose: to represent the peoples of the Member States.

Seats:

Germany	99
France, UK, Italy	78 (each)
Poland, Spain	54 (each)
Romania	35
Netherlands	27
Belgium, Czech Republic, Greece, Hungary, Portugal	24 (each)
Sweden	19
Austria, Bulgaria	18 (each)
Denmark, Finland, Slovakia	14 (each)
Ireland, Lithuania	13 (each)
Latvia	9
Slovenia	7
Cyprus, Estonia, Luxembourg	6 (each)
Malta	5
Total	**785**

POWERS AND DUTIES

The powers and duties of the European Parliament can be categorised as follows:

■ supervisory function;

■ participation in legislative process;

■ budgetary function;

■ special powers.

SUPERVISORY FUNCTION

The Commission is politically accountable to the Parliament. The Parliament consequently has a number of powers to hold the Commission accountable:

■ the Commission has to reply orally or in writing to questions put to it by the Parliament (Art 197);

■ the Parliament can demand the resignation of the Commission *en bloc*;

■ the Parliament debates the annual report produced by the Commission;

■ there is a system of Parliamentary Committees which prepare decisions of the Parliament and maintain regular contact with the Commission when the Parliament is not sitting;

- members of the Commission participate in Parliamentary debates;
- the Parliament uses its budgetary powers to hold the Commission accountable.

The Parliament also exercises supervisory powers over the Council. Although not obliged to do so, the Council replies to both written and, through the President of the relevant Council formation, oral questions. Council Presidents are invited to appear before Parliamentary committees and attend plenary sessions to give the views of Council or give an account of Council business. A problem in supervising the Council arises from the fact that it represents the national interest and therefore speaks with a discordant voice.

The TEU gave additional supervisory powers to the Parliament:

- it has the right to set up temporary Committees of Inquiry to investigate 'alleged contraventions or maladministration in the implementation of Community law' (except where the matter is *sub judice*);
- any citizen of the Union or any resident of a Member State has the right to petition the European Parliament on a matter within Community competence which affects him directly;
- an Ombudsman will be empowered to receive complaints concerning instances of maladministration in the activities of Community institutions or bodies (except the ECJ and Court of First Instance).

The jurisdiction of the ombudsman was extended to the reformed third pillar of the European Union, that of Police and Judicial Co-operation in Criminal Matters, by the Treaty of Amsterdam.

PARTICIPATION IN THE LEGISLATIVE PROCESS
There are four components of the legislative process: consultation procedure; co-operation procedure; co-decision procedure; and assent. The relevant procedure and consequently the Parliament's involvement in the process is governed by the Treaties.

PROCEDURE WITHOUT CONSULTATION
The most significant area in which legislation can be adopted without any involvement of the European Parliament is that of the common commercial

policy. All that Art 133 requires is a Commission proposal and adoption by the Council, acting by a qualified majority. In practice, the Commission usually suggests that the Parliament be consulted on an optional basis and the Council frequently follows this advice.

CONSULTATIVE FUNCTION

One of the Parliament's main functions has traditionally been to advise and be consulted on proposed legislation. Prior to the SEA, the Treaties gave the European Parliament a right to be consulted only in the legislative process. The tendency is to limit the use of the consultation procedure to economic sectors of special political sensitivity in the Member States, or to matters felt to impinge directly on sovereignty. The areas where the consultation procedure is used include: provisions relating to aspects of environmental policy, harmon- isation of indirect taxation, decisions on how a European Union citizen can exercise his right to vote and stand in municipal and European elections, visa policy and provisions relating to the Statute of the European System of Central Banks.

The Commission forwards a proposal to the Council, which in turn forwards it to the Parliament for its opinion. The proposal is passed to the appropriate Parliamentary Committee before a plenary session of Parliament gives its opinion. There is no obligation on the Commission or the Council to follow this opinion. However, failure to consult the Parliament where there is a Treaty requirement so to do is a breach of an 'essential procedural requirement' and the legislation will be annulled (*Roquette v Council* [1980] and *Maizena v Council* [1980]).

The Parliament must be reconsulted if the Commission amends the proposal or the Council intends to use its own power of amendment and the resulting text, considered as a whole, differs in substance from the one which was the subject of the original request for an opinion (Case C-65/90 *European Parliament v Council* [1992]).

There is no requirement on the Commission to consult the Parliament while formulating a proposal. However, the Parliament can use its supervisory power over the Commission to indirectly influence the Council in the consultation procedure. The Council takes its decisions on the basis of Commission pro- posals. The Commission would want its proposals to enjoy broad support from the Parliament, as the former is accountable to the latter. In this indirect way, the Parliament can bring pressure to bear to ensure that its opinions are respected.

Certain provisions of the Treaty require the Council, before taking a decision, to consult, either in addition to or instead of the European Parliament, other Community institutions or bodies. Previously, the only bodies to be consulted were the Economic and Social Committee and the Court of Auditors in relation to financial legislation. The TEU extends the range of bodies from which opinions must be sought. In particular, it provides for a Committee of Regions.

Consultation procedure

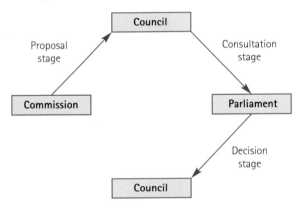

Procedure referred to in Art 252 (co-operation procedure)

The SEA introduced a new legislative procedure which gave the Parliament greater say over legislation. This involves two readings on the part of the Council and the Parliament. The areas where the co-operation procedure are used now are mainly concerned with Economic and Monetary Union.

The Council, acting by a qualified majority and after obtaining the opinion of the European Parliament, can adopt the act if it agrees with the European Parliament's amendments or if the European Parliament does not propose any amendments.

Co-operation procedure

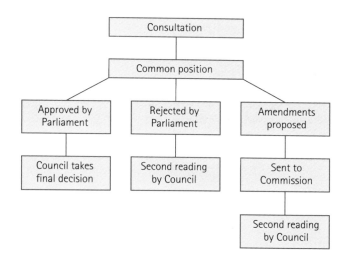

If the Council is unable to agree on the European Parliament's amendments, it will adopt a 'common position' which is communicated to the European Parliament. This sets in motion a second reading. If the European Parliament approves the common position or does not take a decision within three months, the act is adopted.

If the European Parliament is opposed to the measure, it can only be adopted by the Council if it acts unanimously.

If the Parliament proposes an amendment and the amendment is adopted by the Commission, the Council can only reject it if it acts unanimously.

Co-decision procedure

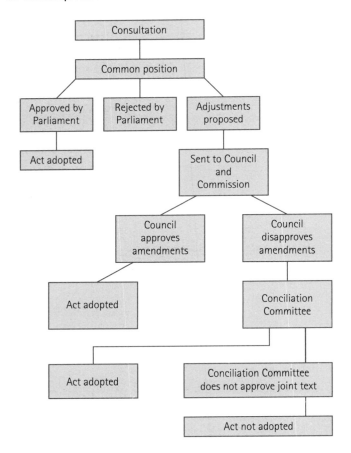

Technically, it is incorrect to call this procedure 'co-decision', as it does not give the Parliament equal rights of approval over the legislative procedure. Nevertheless, the Parliament's influence over legislation has been increased still further where the procedure has been used. The correct term is 'Article 251 procedure'.

The procedure is for the Commission to send its proposals to both the Council and the Parliament.

The ToA has strengthened the powers of the European Parliament in relation to the co-decision procedure. If the Council and the Parliament are unable to agree a joint text in the Conciliation Committee, the act is not now adopted. In effect, the European Parliament has a power of veto.

The procedure under Art 251 applies to most important legislation produced by the EC.

Where the Parliament proposes amendments, the amended text is sent to both the Council and the Commission. The Council can within three months (which can be extended by common accord by one month) accept and adopt this amended proposal (acting by a qualified majority, except in respect of amendments on which the Commission has delivered a negative opinion, where the Council must act unanimously), or if it is not accepted, then the Conciliation Committee can be convened to agree a joint text.

The Council acting on its own or in alliance with the Commission can no longer override the wishes of the Parliament.

Assent procedure

The assent procedure was introduced by the SEA. Originally, the Parliament's approval was required for the admission of new members and for the conclusion of association agreements. The category of agreements to which it applies was considerably enlarged by the TEU. It now applies to more international agreements and, in certain cases, the legislative sphere, including:

- acts defining the tasks, policy objectives and organisation of structural funds;

- decision to set up a Cohesion Fund;

- various aspects of the functioning of the European Central Bank;

- amendment of certain provisions of the Statute of European System of Central Banks (ESCB).

LACK OF TRANSPARENCY

The variants on the number of decision making procedures have been criticised for creating a lack of transparency. The number of different procedures makes it very difficult for laypersons/citizens to understand.

BUDGETARY POWERS

The Parliament's powers in relation to the budget were significantly increased by the Budgetary Treaties of 1970 and 1975. As a result of the latter Treaty, the Parliament now jointly exercises control over the budget with the Council, although since 1988 it does so within the context of 'budgetary discipline'.

The budget is drafted by the Commission and is made up of two parts – compulsory expenditure and non-compulsory expenditure.

The Council has the final say over 'compulsory expenditure', which consists mainly of expenditure on the Common Agricultural Policy, and the Parliament has the final say over 'non-compulsory expenditure' which relates mainly to social and regional policy, research and aid to non-European Union countries such as Russia and countries in Eastern Europe.

PARLIAMENT AND THE ECJ

Historically, the Parliament has been weak, and it has constantly been attempting to extend its role and increase its power and influence. One method developed by the Parliament to put pressure on the Council to take decisions has been to take cases to the ECJ.

Failure to act: In *European Parliament v Council* [1985], the ECJ held that the Parliament could bring proceedings against the Council under Art 175 (now Art 232) for failure to act when the Council had been in breach of its Treaty obligations by failing to adopt a common transport policy. Although the Court held that the Council should have acted, it was not prepared to say what the content of the Council's provisions should have been.

Action to annul: Although the right to bring an action for failure to act was granted readily, there was initially far more reluctance on the part of the ECJ to allow the Parliament privileged status in bringing actions for the other type of judicial review, that of 'actions to annul' under Art 230. A long line of cases, for example, Case 377/87 *European Parliament v Council* [1988] and Case 302/87

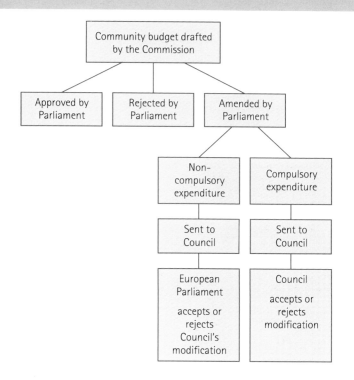

European Parliament v Council [1988], held that the European Parliament did not have power to bring annulment proceedings. Eventually, it was held in Case 70/88 *European Parliament v Council* (*Chernobyl* case) [1990] that the Parliament could bring an action to annul where there had been an infringement of the Parliament's rights and the action was taken in order to safeguard those rights.

Actions against Parliament: The Parliament can be a defendant as well as a complainant before the ECJ. The original intention of the Treaty drafters was that the Parliament should be liable for its decisions in staff cases. Liability has since been extended and the ECJ has held that the Parliament can be a source of 'justiciable acts' and can be sued under Art 230 (actions to annul). This has led to other Community institutions and individuals (other than staff) challenging the decisions of the European Parliament.

So, in *Parti Ecologiste 'Les Verts' v European Parliament* [1983], a French political party was able to obtain annulment of European Parliament Bureau decisions concerning the distribution of funds to political parties who participated in the 1984 Euro elections.

Similarly, in Case 34/86 *Council v European Parliament* [1986], the Council obtained a ruling that the decision of the President of the Parliament declaring the 1986 budget adopted was illegal.

This does not mean that all acts of the Parliament are 'justiciable'. The reason the ECJ included acts of the Parliament within actions to annul was to ensure that all legally binding acts were capable of judicial review. In *Group of the European Right v European Parliament* [1985], a decision by the President of the European Parliament declaring admissible a motion for the setting up of a Committee of Inquiry into the rise of fascism and racism was not capable of challenge.

Historical development of the European Parliament's powers
Examination questions frequently ask for an historical analysis of the development of the European Parliament's powers. It is important to keep certain key dates in mind.

1957 – Founding Treaties: These give the Parliament the right to advise and be consulted, and supervise the Commission. A small number of special powers are also granted.

1970–75 – Budgetary Treaties: These give the Parliament: power to reject draft budget in its entirety; final say on non-compulsory expenditure; power to propose amendments to compulsory expenditure.

1979 – Direct elections: Not an increase in powers but an enhancement of the Parliament's moral authority which encouraged the Parliament to use existing draconian powers, that is, rejection of draft budget to pressurise other institutions.

1986 – Single European Act: Introduction of co-operation procedure. Assent to new members and association agreements. But greater implementation powers for Commission.

1992 – Treaty on European Union: More consultative powers. Co-operation procedure extended to new powers. Introduction of procedure referred to in Art 189b (now Art 251), 'the co-decision procedure'. Assent extended to new areas including legislative field. Power of veto over appointment of new Commissioners. 'Committees of Inquiry'. Right to 'request' proposals from Commission. Right of citizens of European Union to petition Parliament. Power to appoint Ombudsman. Consultative role in relation to the Foreign and Security and Justice and Home Affairs pillars of the Union.

1997 – Treaty of Amsterdam: This sees a further extension of the European Parliament's powers. Its position in the co-decision procedure is strengthened.

The European Parliament began as a very weak body but has steadily been increasing its powers. Successive Treaties have augmented its powers, with the possible exception of the SEA. Bieber *et al* (1991) 23 CML Rev 767 argue that, although powers are increased by the Single European Act, in some ways, particularly in relation to the decision making process, the overall effect was neutral. As the Parliament has certain 'horizontal' powers over the whole of the Treaty, it was argued that the effect of the Treaty on the Parliament could only be assessed by considering changes in the powers of the other institutions. The increase in the implementing powers of the Commission affected the Parliament, first, as the committee system (whereby the Council retains some measure of control over implementing legislation) affects the Parliament in its supervisory capacity and, secondly, because the committee system weakens the Parliament's budgetary powers.

The Treaty of Lisbon aims to strengthen the European Parliament's legislative powers by extending the co-decision procedure to further policy areas.

Although the Parliament gives the outward appearance of being like any other

Parliament, the reality is quite different. Despite being the sole Community institution which has its members elected on a Euro-wide level, sovereignty still has a role to play. There are *pro rata* far fewer MEPs for the larger Member States than the smaller ones. Also the Executive is not sustained in power by having a majority in Parliament as is the case in the UK with the Government of the day having a majority in the House of Commons.

The Parliament has weak supervisory powers over the Council. The Council's decisions are taken in secret and its lack of accountability has lead to what has been called a 'democratic deficit' in the Community.

THE COURTS

EUROPEAN COURT OF JUSTICE
Under Art 220, the function of the ECJ is to ensure that in the interpretation and application of the Treaty the law is observed.

Composition: judges and Advocates General
The ECJ consists of one judge from each Member State, so presently there are 27 judges. The judges are assisted by eight Advocates General. The number of Advocates General may be increased by the Council acting unanimously if the ECJ requests this. They must be independent and possess the qualifications required for the appointment to the highest judicial office in their respective countries or be jurisconsults of recognised competence. They are appointed by common accord of the governments of the Member States for a term of six years, expiring at intervals of three years, although they may be reappointed. A judge can only be removed during his term if all the judges and Advocates General are agreed.

The judges elect a President of the ECJ from among their number for a renewable term of three years.

The ECJ may sit in plenary session or in chambers which consist of three to five judges. The Court sits in plenary session in all cases where an institution or Member State so requests.

The Advocate General's position is curious to UK lawyers. The role was based on the *commissaire du gouvernement* in the French Conseil d'État. He has the same status as a judge and his duty is to present an impartial and reasoned opinion on the case, prior to the judges' deliberations. There is a slight resemblance to the *amicus curiae* in English law. An *amicus curiae* is a 'friend of the court' who gives the court the benefit of his views on a question of law. A major difference between the two is that the Advocate General, in contrast to the *amicus curiae*, does not represent a particular interest and is completely independent. An opinion is usually, but not always, followed by the Court, and it has no legal force. The Advocate General can only hope to influence the Court through the force of his judgment, as he does not take part in the judges' deliberations. It has been suggested that as the ECJ was a court of both first and last instance when it was established, the Advocate General's opinion provided an in-built appeal mechanism to the ECJ's deliberations.

Procedure

Procedure before the ECJ has four stages (although the second is often omitted):

1   written proceedings;
2   investigation or preparatory inquiry;
3   oral proceedings;
4   judgment.

Proceedings are commenced by written application. The application can be in any of the official or working languages of the Community. If the applicant is a Member State or individual, the general rule is that the applicant has the choice of language. If the action is against a Member State, the defendant chooses the language of the case. French is the working language of the Court.

The defendant serves a defence in reply to the application, and it is possible for the applicant to serve a reply.

One of the judges is assigned the role of judge *rapporteur* and will study the papers relating to the case, which will also have been examined by the Advocate General assigned to the case. After close of pleadings the ECJ may decide that a preliminary inquiry is needed. Although this is rare, the decision will be based on the judge *rapporteur*'s preliminary report and the views of the Advocate General.

Prior to the oral hearing, the judge *rapporteur* issues a report summarising the facts of the case and the parties' arguments. There are tight time limits on counsel during oral proceedings and the main speeches are not normally interrupted by questions. The Advocate General's opinion is also given orally but usually at a different time from the counsel's arguments.

Only one judgment is produced after the judge *rapporteur* has produced another report on the law relating to the case. Deliberations are in secret and the requirement to produce one judgment means that it is often anodyne where there has been disagreement between the judges, as it has to be sufficiently vague to promote agreement between all the judges. Judgments also tend to be bland, for linguistic reasons.

The Court is bound to include in its judgment a decision as to costs. The usual rule is that the losing party must pay the winning party's costs, but there can be exceptions such as staff cases, where the employer normally pays. Costs in preliminary references are normally reserved to the national court.

The Court can also grant legal aid. It will do so where it seems just and equitable to do so and it can be granted even where it it would not be available in national proceedings.

Jurisdiction

The jurisdiction of the ECJ has been conferred on it by Art 220 as follows:

- Actions against Community institutions/judicial review of a Community institution's acts. Art 230 gives Member States, the Commission, the Council and the European Parliament, the locus standi to seek judicial review by the ECJ of another Community institution's acts. For example, the European Parliament could question the legality of a binding act of the Commission and seek annulment of that act. There are four specific grounds on which such judicial review may be sought: lack of competence; infringement of an essential procedural requirement; infringement of the Treaties; misuse of power. Natural and legal persons have locus standi to seek such judicial review by the CFI but in limited circumstances only, e.g. they may challenge a decision addressed to them which is of direct and individual concern. Most cases brought by undertakings involve a challenge of a Commission decision relating to the undertaking's liability for a breach of competition law (see below jurisdiction of the CFI)

● Other actions against Community institutions include actions for failure to act (Art 232); actions for damages (Arts 235 and 288) and at one time staff cases, which are now dealt with by the Court of First Instance (CFI).

■ Preliminary rulings under Art 234 (see Chapter 4).

■ Actions brought either by the Commission (Art 226) or a Member State (Art 227) against another Member State for failure to fulfil Community obligations.

■ Since 1989, the ECJ has had an appellate jurisdiction and hears appeals from the CFI on points of law from undertakings which have been fined as a result of Commission decisions relating to competition law.

■ The Court can also give advisory opinions under Art 300 on an agreement between the European Union and third countries or international organisations.

Quasi-legislative role

One of the striking features of the ECJ is its approach to interpretation. The ECJ employs a purposive, or teleological, approach and interprets legislation in accordance with its aims and purposes. In this approach, the Court is guided by the principle of *effet utile*, or effectiveness, and is constantly striving to ensure that their interpretation leads to a furthering of the integration process by ensuring that the European legal order functions more effectively. It is argued that, as a result, the judges are not being creative at all; they are precluded from performing a legislative function, as they are tied to the aims of the Treaties and are therefore limited in their policy choices. A problem with this analysis is that there is no unanimous agreement between the Member States as to the form integration, and consequently the policy choices, should take.

The teleological approach has had several important consequences. First, it has lead to a constitutionalisation of the founding Treaties. This constitution is said to rest on the 'twin pillars' of direct effect and supremacy. (See Chapter 2.)

The ECJ has defined the powers of the respective institutions and the competence of the Community. In *Commission v Council* (*ERTA* case) [1971], it was held that the Community had competence to enter into an agreement with third countries when policy making in a certain area has been handed over to the Community.

The principle of *effet utile* in combination with Art 10, under which Member States agree to fulfil their Community obligations, have been used by the ECJ to develop an interpretive obligation on Member States (*Von Colson and Kamman* [1986] and *Marleasing* [1990]) and to develop the safeguarding of rights through the availability of compensation in the event of the State breaching those rights (*Francovich* [1990]). (See Chapter 2.)

Easson feels that the activist stage of the ECJ has come to an end and, now that the general principles of the legal order are established, further developments will depend on the legislators ('Legal approaches to European integration' (1986)). On the other hand, Ramussen, in *On Law and Policy in the European Court of Justice* (1986), feels that the ECJ has been unnecessarily activist in the past and will continue to be so in the future. Rasmussen and Snyder (*Effectiveness of EC law: institutions, processes, tools and techniques* (1993)) see a danger in the ECJ's activist role, as it lacks legitimacy to perform such a role and there has been a lack of popular involvement in the development of the legal order.

COURT OF FIRST INSTANCE

The case load of the ECJ has increased dramatically since the inception of the Community. It can now take over two years to receive a judgment. To help alleviate the workload, the Single European Act 1986 provided for the establishment of a CFI. The CFI was established by Council Decision 88/591 and began hearing cases in 1989.

The CFI consists of 27 judges and sits in chambers of three or five judges, or occasionally in plenary session. Article 225 provides that, to qualify as judges, 'members of [the] court shall be chosen from persons whose independence is beyond doubt and who possess the ability required for appointment to judicial office'. There is a President of the Court who is elected from amongst the judges. The CFI has its own Registry and the members of the court have their own personal staff but otherwise all other services are provided by the staff of the ECJ and the CFI is 'attached' to the ECJ.

The CFI's jurisdiction is as follows:

■ staff cases;

■ actions brought by natural and legal persons against a Community institution under Arts 230 and 232 relating to the implementation of competition rules applicable to undertakings;

■ all claims brought by 'natural and legal persons' under Arts 230 and 232 (including anti-dumping cases);

■ Following the entry into force of the Treaty of Nice, the CFI has jurisdiction to hear preliminary rulings. See Chapter 4.

The competition and staff cases take up most of the CFI's time. Both types of case are fact-based, and were therefore thought suitable to transfer to a different court as they would be the most likely to alleviate the workload of the ECJ.

It is possible to appeal a decision of the CFI to the ECJ, on points of law only, on three grounds:

1   lack of competence of the CFI;
2   breach of procedure before the CFI which adversely affects the interests of the applicant;
3   infringement of Community law by the CFI.

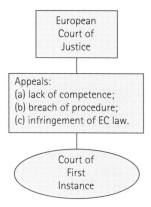

If the ECJ finds that an appeal is successful, it quashes the CFI's judgment. It can then give final judgment itself or refer the case back to the CFI for judgment.

Kennedy (1989) 14 EL Rev 7 saw a danger that if a high proportion of CFI decisions ended in appeals, then there would be a minimal reduction in the ECJ's caseload. However, even if this were to occur, there would still be a saving in time for the ECJ as the facts have already been determined by the CFI, leaving the ECJ to apply the law.

Since the inception of the CFI, there has been little reduction in the waiting time before the ECJ, as it coincided with an increase in cases.

You should now be confident that you would be able to tick all of the boxes on the checklist at the beginning of this chapter. To check your knowledge of Community institutions why not visit the companion website and take the Multiple Choice Question test. Check your understanding of the terms and vocabulary used in this chapter with the flashcard glossary.

4

Preliminary rulings

Understand the purposes of the preliminary reference procedure ☐

Appreciate how the procedure has been used to develop Community law ☐

Understand what is meant by 'a court or tribunal' in this context ☐

Know when a court has a discretion to make a preliminary reference and when it has an obligation to refer ☐

Identify when a preliminary reference would not be necessary ☐

Consider whether the ECJ can refuse to hear a reference ☐

Understand the effect of a preliminary ruling ☐

Be aware of proposals for reform of the preliminary reference procedure ☐

PRELIMINARY REFERENCES

Article 234 of the EC Treaty gives the ECJ jurisdiction to give preliminary references on questions of interpretation and validity of Community law at the request of the national courts of a Member State. The procedure is for the national court to hear the case, and when it encounters problems relating to interpretation of the Treaties or the interpretation or validity of acts of the institutions of the Community, e.g. regulations, directives, decisions, opinions and recommendations, the case is referred to the ECJ. It should be stressed that the validity of the Treaties cannot be questioned. After a ruling, the ECJ returns the case to the national court for it to be applied to the facts of the case. So, the case starts and ends in the national courts. Art 234, para 2 provides that 'any court or tribunal' has a discretion to request a preliminary reference, but a court against whose decision there is no judicial remedy is obliged to make a preliminary reference under Art 234(3).

PURPOSE OF PRELIMINARY REFERENCES

There are four main purposes of preliminary references:

1 Uniformity of interpretation throughout Member States

The principle of supremacy ensures that Community law prevails over national law where the two conflict. This principle would be undermined if the national courts were free to interpret Community law in their own way with the inevitable result that the law would differ from State to State. Preliminary references ensure that there is an authoritative source for interpretation. Although it is possible for secondary legislation to be annulled, preliminary references ensure that only the ECJ can do this, again to avoid discrepancies from State to State.

2 Familiarise national courts with workings of European legal order

This has influenced the ECJ's approach to requests for references. In the early days, the ECJ was keen to encourage requests, as without them it would be unable to develop the legal order. Consequently, the ECJ initially was not formalistic in its approach and did not make specifications about the timing or the form of the request. The ECJ also emphasised that the process involved an equal division of labour, and that it was not higher in

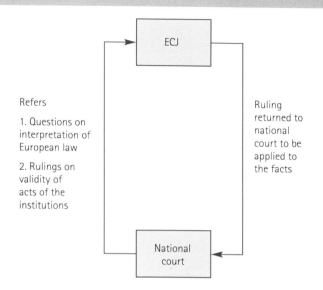

Refers

1. Questions on interpretation of European law

2. Rulings on validity of acts of the institutions

Ruling returned to national court to be applied to the facts

any hierarchy to the national court but was performing an equal but different role alongside the national courts. This approach was successful and the ECJ currently has a large backlog of requests.

3 Develop European legal order

The ECJ has used preliminary references to develop the legal order and constitutionalise the Treaties. So, it was through requests for preliminary references that the ECJ was able to develop the 'twin pillars' of direct effect (*Van Gend en Loos* [1963]) and supremacy (*Costa v ENEL* [1964]).

The ECJ has also been able to extend the scope and effectiveness of the legal order through a combination of preliminary references and Art 10 of the EC Treaty. In this way, it has created an interpretive obligation on Member States to ensure that national courts interpret national legislation in accordance with the aims and purposes of directives (*Von Colson and Kamman* [1984]; *Marleasing* [1992]); individuals receive compensation where they have suffered damage as a result of a Member State breaching its Community obligations (*Francovich* [1992]); and there are effective procedural remedies to ensure the protection of Community rights (*Factortame* [1990]; *Emmott* [1991]; *Zuckerfabrik* [1991]).

4 Rulings on direct effect

Preliminary references have also been used to determine whether Treaty provisions and secondary legislation satisfy the criteria for direct effect and can consequently be relied upon by individuals before national courts.

WHAT IS A COURT OR TRIBUNAL?

Article 234 permits only references from a 'court or tribunal'. Essentially, the test for 'court or tribunal' is a wide one and includes any body with official backing which exercises a judicial function according to the normal rules of adversarial procedure and has the power to give binding determinations of legal rights and obligations, independent of the parties in dispute (*Dorsch Consult* [1997]). It is not decisive that the body is recognised as a court under national law (*Corbiau* [1993]).

In *Nederlandse Spoorwegen* [1973], the Dutch Raad van State was held to be a court or tribunal within the meaning of Art 234. In theory, an application for judicial review in the Netherlands is decided by the Crown but is in practice based on the advice of the Raad van State. The ECJ took a pragmatic view and found that the Raad van State was a court or tribunal within Art 234.

In *Vassen* [1966], a reference from a body which was an arbitration tribunal but whose members were appointed by the Dutch Minister for Social Security and operated in accordance with ordinary adversarial procedure did come within Art 234.

Similarly, in *Broekmeulen* [1981], a Dutch body called the Appeals Committee for General Medicine heard appeals from a medical disciplinary tribunal. The ability to practise as a medical practitioner was dependent on registration with the Committee and one-third of the Appeals Committee's members were appointed by the Dutch Government. This too was held to be a 'court or tribunal' within the meaning of Art 234.

A tribunal which mixes judicial functions with other functions was still held to be a tribunal within the meaning of Art 234 in *Pretore di Salo v Persons Unknown* [1987].

The ECJ will accept requests for references from any body satisfying the criteria, regardless of whether or not the body bears the name 'court' or 'tribunal'. Thus, reference requests have been accepted from Italy's Bar Council (*Gebhard* [1996]), Sweden's Universities' Appeals Board (*Abrahamsson & Anderson v Fogelqvist* [2000]) and the UK's Immigration Adjudicator (*El-Yassini* [1999] and *Kaba* [2000]) and Social Security Commissioner (*O'Flynn* [1996]).

In *De coster v College des Bourgmestres et Echevins de Watermael-Boitsfort* [2000], the ECJ stated that when determining whether a body is a court or tribunal 'the court takes account of a number of factors, such as whether the body is established by law, whether it is permanent, whether its jurisdiction is compulsory, whether its procedure is inter partes, whether it applies rules of law and whether it is independent'.

The position is unclear as to whether international courts such as the European Court of Human Rights would be able to make a reference.

Lack of jurisdiction

A commercial arbitration tribunal was held not to come within Art 234 in *Nordsee v Reederei Mond* [1982], and this rule applies even if the award of the tribunal can be enforced through the courts.

The ECJ also refused to accept requests for references from a public prosecutor in *Criminal Proceedings against X* [1996] – a prosecutor clearly does not exercise judicial functions – and from the Swedish revenue board in *Victoria Film* [1998], on the basis that its functions were purely administrative with no powers to resolve legal disputes.

WHEN TO REFER

The question of the national court's timing of a reference can only be understood in the context of the ECJ's changing policy in relation to preliminary references. In the initial stages, the ECJ was keen to encourage references, as without them it would be unable to familiarise national courts with their approach and develop the legal order. Emphasis was placed on the co-operative aspects of the procedure and the fact that there was an equal division of labour between the ECJ and the national court. As a result of this policy, the ECJ was relaxed about the timing of references. Similarly, the ECJ has not been formalistic in its approach and, in the past, if the question had not been properly asked, the ECJ reformulated the question and asked itself the question that should have been asked.

In *R v Henn and Darby* [1981], the ECJ said that it was preferable but not essential for the facts of a case to be decided prior to a reference. The reason for its preference was that it wished to consider as many aspects of the case as possible before giving its ruling.

In *Creamery Milk Suppliers* [1980], the Irish High Court requested a ruling without first considering the facts. The ECJ accepted the reference and said that the timing of the reference was entirely at the national court's discretion.

The ECJ became a victim of its success over the working of this co-operative policy. It has developed a backlog of cases and it now takes, on average, 20–24 months for a preliminary reference to be heard by the ECJ. The ECJ no longer feels the need to encourage national courts to make references, and in recent cases it has been prepared to take a firmer line on the timing of references.

In both *Pretore di Genova v Banchero* [1993] and *Telemarsicabruzzo SpA v Circostel* [1993], the ECJ held that the national court must define the factual and legal framework in which the questions arise before making a preliminary reference.

In both cases, the ECJ said that the questions referred were so vague that they could not be answered. In both cases, the ECJ emphasised its role in Art 234 proceedings, which is to provide a ruling that would be useful to a national court in the administration of justice. As both cases involved competition law, the facts were particularly complicated, and this heightened the need for a clear description of the facts.

In December 1996, a *Note for Guidance on References by National Courts for Preliminary Rulings* was published by the ECJ. The Note is for guidance only and has no binding or interpretative effect.

In the Note, it is said that the order for reference should contain a statement of reasons which is succinct but sufficiently complete to give the ECJ, and those to whom it must be notified, a clear understanding of the factual and legal context of the main proceedings.

In particular, it should include:

- a statement of the facts which are essential to a full understanding of the legal significance of the main proceedings;

- an exposition of the national law which may be applicable;

- a statement of the reasons which have prompted the national court to refer the question or questions to the ECJ; and

- where appropriate, a summary of the arguments of the parties.

The aim should be to put the ECJ in a position to give the national court an answer which will be of assistance to it.

The court issued a revised Note in 2005 regarding the point in national proceedings when a preliminary reference should be made. It stated 'A national court or tribunal may refer a question to the Court of Justice for a preliminary ruling as soon as it finds that a ruling on the point or points of interpretation or validity is necessary to enable it to give judgment; it is the national court which is in the best position to decide at what stage of the proceedings such a question should be referred.' The Note continued that 'a decision to seek a preliminary ruling should be taken when the proceedings have reached a stage at which the national court is able to define the factual and legal context of the question, so that the Court has available to it all the information necessary to check, where appropriate that Community law applies to the main proceedings'. It may also be in the interests of justice to refer a question for a preliminary ruling only after both sides have been heard.

DISCRETION TO REFER

Under Art 234(2), any court or tribunal of a Member State has a discretion to make a reference to the ECJ. This right cannot be curtailed by national law: *Second Rheinmuhlen Case* [1974], and it cannot be fettered by a regulation of the Communities: *BRT-Sabam* [1974].

Principles under which a British court should exercise its discretion were originally indicated by Lord Denning MR in *Bulmer v Bollinger* [1974]:

- The decision must be necessary to enable the English court to give judgment.

- In deciding whether the reference is necessary, account must be taken of the following factors:

- Is the answer to the question conclusive of the case?

- Is there a previous ruling by the ECJ on the issue?

- Is the provision *acte clair*? (see below)

- Have the facts of the case been decided?

If the court decides that a decision is necessary, it must still consider the following factors:

- delay;

- the difficulty and importance of the point;

- expense;

- the burden on the ECJ;

- the wishes of the parties;

- difficulty in framing the question in sufficiently clear terms to benefit from a ruling.

These criteria have been attacked on the grounds that they are unduly restrictive and delaying, because the expense and burden on the parties may, in fact, increase if a referral has to be made by a higher court.

The correct approach was redefined by Sir Thomas Bingham MR in *R v International Stock Exchange of the UK and the Republic of Ireland ex p Else* [1993]. In his view, three steps need to be taken in deciding whether to make a referral:

- first, find the facts;

- secondly, consider whether the Community law provision is critical to the outcome;

- thirdly, consider whether the court could resolve the provision of Community law with complete confidence.

In addition, the court must be mindful of four factors when making its decision:

- the differences between national law and Community law;

■ the pitfalls of entering into an unfamiliar field;

■ the need for uniform interpretation;

■ the advantage enjoyed by the ECJ in interpreting Community legislation.

It was held in *Trent Taverns Ltd v Sykes* [1999] that the Court of Appeal could, in the exercise of its discretion, make a reference to the ECJ in a case where the relevant point of Community law had already been decided by the Court of Appeal, as the ordinary principles of *stare decisis* were not applicable to such references.

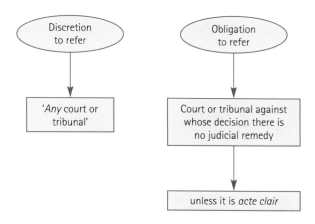

OBLIGATION TO REFER

Article 234(3) provides that a court or tribunal against whose decision there is no judicial remedy is obliged to make a reference to the ECJ. There are two differing views as to what is meant by the phrase 'a court or tribunal against whose decision there is no judicial remedy':

1   'Abstract theory': it can only mean the highest court in the land. In the UK, this would be the House of Lords only. This view was supported by Lord Denning in *Bulmer v Bollinger*.

2   'Concrete theory': it includes courts which are judging in final instance in that particular case. For example, in order to appeal from the Court of Appeal to the House of Lords it is necessary to have leave. If leave is not

forthcoming, then the Court of Appeal is the highest court in that particular case. There are comments supporting this theory in *Costa v ENEL* [1964]. In *Hagen* [1980], the Court of Appeal held that it is bound to make a reference under Art 234 if leave to appeal to the House of Lords is not obtainable.

However, in *Kenny Roland Lyckeskog* [2000], a Swedish district court asked the ECJ whether it had an obligation to refer as an appeal from its decision to the Swedish Supreme Court would only be made if the Swedish Supreme Court stated that such an appeal was admissible. The ECJ held that the possibility of an appeal to the Supreme Court meant that the district court could not be considered a court of last resort for the purposes of Art 234.

In these circumstances, it seems that the English Court of Appeal would not be considered to be a court 'against whose decisions there is no judicial remedy'.

In theory, the Commission can bring enforcement proceedings against a Member State whose highest court does not make a preliminary reference, but in practice it does not do so.

Interim proceedings

In *Hoffman-La Roche v Centrafarm* [1978], the question arose as to whether an interim order, given in interlocutory proceedings against which there was no judicial remedy but which could be considered again in the main proceedings, was a decision against which there was no judicial remedy. The ECJ emphasised that preliminary references could be made but that there was no obligation to make a reference when the matter could be considered again in the main proceedings.

Acte clair

The ECJ has sanctioned the use of *acte clair* from French law, subject to conditions, where the answer to the question is clear and free from doubt. If an act is *acte clair*, even a court that comes within Art 234(3) is freed from its obligation to refer.

In *CILFT* [1982], the doctrine of *acte clair* was accepted by the ECJ, when it said that an application would not be 'necessary' if:

■ the question of Community law was irrelevant;

■ the provision had already been interpreted by the ECJ;

■ the correct application is so obvious that it leaves no room for doubt.

In addition to these criteria, the national court must also be convinced that the answer would be equally obvious to a court in another Member State as well as to the ECJ. The national court must compare the different versions of the text in the various Community languages. It must also bear in mind that legal concepts and terminology do not necessarily have the same meaning in Community law as in national law.

These last criteria deprive the doctrine of *acte clair* of much of its practical effect. The national judge must not only be satisfied that the provision is free from doubt in his own language but he must peruse the text in the other official languages of the EC and, taking into account the different legal concepts in the different jurisdictions, still be satisfied that the matter is free from doubt. This is an immense challenge, even for the most accomplished linguist. This challenge became even more daunting in May 2004 when 10 new Member States joined the EU, bringing with them several new official languages (Czech, Estonian, Hungarian, Latvian, Lithuanian, Maltese, Polish, Slovak and Slovene). In fact, it is difficult to see how any conscientious judge in the expanded EU could ever honestly conclude that a provision in Community legislation bore the same meaning when read by judges in 27 countries using 22 different languages. The narrowness with which the doctrine has been drawn is a reflection of the advantage that the ECJ has over national courts in interpreting legislation and comparing the different texts.

▶ CILFT (Case 283/81)

It was alleged that duties imposed by Italian law were contrary to an EC regulation. The Italian Ministry of Health urged the Italian court against whose decision there was no judicial remedy not to refer the matter to the ECJ as the answer to the question to be referred was obvious.

The ECJ stated that it may not be necessary to make a reference where the question of EC law is irrelevant, where the question has already been interpreted by the ECJ and where the correct interpretation is obvious (an *acte clair*).

It was held in *Da Costa* [1963] that a national court is free to make another preliminary reference, even where the question has been the subject of a previous ruling or where it is *acte clair*.

Validity

In *Foto-Frost* [1987], it was held by the ECJ that national courts could not find Community legislation invalid. So the *acte clair* doctrine cannot apply to questions of invalidity, but it is possible for national courts to find Community acts valid. An exception exists in cases of interlocutory proceedings, where national courts, for reasons of urgency, can rule that Community acts are invalid on an interim basis. In *Zuckerfabrik Süderdithmarschen AG v Hauptzollamt Itzehoe* [1991], it was held that a Community act could be declared temporarily invalid.

The ECJ will not overrule a provision of national law in a preliminary reference, but it can say that a rule of national law is inapplicable in a Community context by providing guidance on the correct interpretation of Community law.

Can the ECJ refuse to hear a reference?

In recent years, this has been one of the most vexed questions in relation to preliminary references and is a popular topic with examiners.

The ECJ will decline to hear a reference when it falls outside Art 234. If the reference is not made by a court or tribunal, as in *Nordsee* [1982], *Criminal Proceedings Against X* [1996] and *Victoria Film* [1998], then it will decline to hear a case.

If the reference is nothing to do with Community law, the ECJ will decline the reference: *Alderblum* [1975]. The fact that the reference has nothing to do with Community law does not mean that it will have been without merit. The national judge will be free to apply national law safe in the knowledge that Community law is not relevant.

In *Bacardi-Martini v Newcastle United FC* [2003], the ECJ refused to respond to a requested reference. The case concerned a dispute between the claimant drinks manufacturer and the defendant football club. The claimant alleged that the club had pressurised a third party, Dorna Marketing Ltd, to withdraw adverts for the claimant's products from perimeter advertising hoardings during a UEFA cup match between Newcastle United and Metz, of France.

Newcastle had taken this action because the game was to be televised in France but French law prohibits the advertising of alcohol on television.

The claimant's High Court action alleged that the club had induced Dorna to break its contract with the claimants. The judge referred the case to the ECJ, seeking guidance on the compatibility of the French law with Community law regarding freedom to provide services (Art 49 of the EC Treaty). However, the requested reference was declared inadmissible. The Court stated:

> . . . it is essential for national courts to explain . . . why they consider that a reply to their questions is necessary to enable them to give judgment . . . the Court must display special vigilance when . . . a question is referred to it with a view to permitting the national court to decide whether the legislation of another Member State is in accordance with Community law.

Absence of genuine dispute

In *Foglia v Novello (No 1)* [1980], the questions referred concerned an import tax imposed by the French on the import of wine from Italy. The litigation was between two Italian parties. Foglia was a wine producer who agreed to sell wine to Novello, an exporter. In order to challenge the French tax, a clause was inserted into the contract that Foglia would not have to pay any duties levied by the French authorities, which was in contravention of Community law. The parties were agreed that the tax was illegal and the contractual clause was a device to ensure that the matter could be brought before a court.

The ECJ refused to hear a reference from the Italian court. It felt that an Italian court was attempting to challenge a French tax and this was abusing the preliminary reference procedure, as it was an indirect method of bringing enforcement proceedings. The ECJ declined to hear the reference on the grounds that there was an absence of a genuine dispute between the parties. The case was returned to the Italian court and the judge reformulated the questions and referred the matter again to the ECJ. The ECJ again refused to hear the case in *Foglia v Novello (No 2)* [1981].

The case has been criticised on the grounds that the ECJ had entered into a review of the national court's decision to refer. The purpose of Art 234 is that there should be co-operation between national courts and the ECJ. If the ECJ is to enter into inquiries as to whether the national court's decision to refer is a correct decision, then it is exercising some sort of appellate jurisdiction. The ECJ had always been keen to emphasise that it performs an equal but different role in relation to Art 234 proceedings, but in the *Foglia* cases it suggested, by reviewing decisions of national courts, that it is higher in a hierarchy to national courts.

The approach adopted in the *Foglia* cases has not really been followed in later cases.

> ### ▶ FOGLIA v NOVELLO (Case 104/79)
>
> The parties to the action had inserted a clause in their contract in order to induce the Italian court to seek a ruling that the French tax system for liqueur wines was invalid. The ECJ declined to give a ruling.

Hypothetical questions

In *Mattheus v Doego* [1978], the ECJ refused to hear hypothetical questions relating to the effect that accession to the Community would have on contractual relations of private parties, on the basis that the ECJ cannot determine in advance the outcome of negotiations or the political act resulting in the admission of a State to the Community.

INTERPRETATION AND APPLICATION

There is a division of competence between the ECJ and the national courts. The ECJ's role is to give an authoritative ruling as to the interpretation or validity of the Treaty provision or Community act, while the national courts apply the ruling to the facts of the case. In other words, the ECJ's role is to interpret, while the national court's role is to apply. In *Costa v ENEL* [1964], the ECJ said:

> ... [Art 234] gives the court no jurisdiction either to apply the Treaty to a specific case or to decide upon the validity of a provision of domestic law in relation to the Treaty, as it would be possible for it to do under Art 169 [now Art 226].

The distinction between interpretation and application can be very difficult to make. In addition, an abstract interpretation may not be of assistance to the national court. In the *LTM* case [1966], the national court had informed the ECJ of the facts of the case. When one of the applicants argued that the question was one of application, the ECJ replied:

> Although the Court has no jurisdiction to take cognisance of the application of the Treaty to a specific case, it may extract from the elements of the case those questions of interpretation and validity which alone fall within its jurisdiction.

EFFECT OF A PRELIMINARY REFERENCE

A preliminary reference is binding on the national court which referred the question for consideration (*Milch-Fett und Eierkontor* [1969]).

The Arsenal case

However, in *Arsenal FC v Reed* [2002], the High Court made a landmark decision when it refused to apply a preliminary ruling that the High Court itself had requested. Arsenal objected to the activities of the defendant, whom it accused of selling unofficial memorabilia, principally scarves, bearing trade mark protected words ('Arsenal' and 'Gunners') and symbols (a cannon and shield) without permission. It accused him of breaching its trade marks. The defendant contended that his customers understood that his goods were not official Arsenal memorabilia but were regarded simply as 'badges of support, loyalty or affiliation'. He pointed out that he also sold 'official' Arsenal memorabilia and that notices at his stalls clearly indicated which items were official and which were not. The High Court judge, Laddie J, found as a matter of fact that Reed's unofficial goods 'would not be perceived as indicating' any trade origin (meaning a connection in the course of trade between the goods and the trade mark proprietor) with Arsenal FC. However, he decided to seek a ruling from the ECJ concerning the interpretation of the relevant Community legislation, Directive 89/104. The question was whether someone like Reed had a defence to alleged trade mark infringement if his use of the trade marked words and symbols did 'not indicate trade origin'.

The ECJ held that 'the essential function of a trade mark is to guarantee the identity of origin of the marked goods to the consumer ... by enabling him, without any possibility of confusion, to distinguish the goods from others which have another origin'. (This suggested that there was no breach, given the High Court's findings that customers would not confuse Reed's unofficial goods with Arsenal's official goods.) However, the ECJ went on to make certain findings of fact. It stated that there was 'a clear possibility in the present case' that some of Reed's consumers may interpret the word 'Arsenal' as designating that the goods were official merchandise.

Back in the High Court, Laddie J agreed with Reed that the ECJ had overstepped its jurisdiction in making findings of fact. He therefore applied the Court's reasoning as to the 'function' of a trade mark, but did so in order to achieve the opposite conclusion, ie that there was no breach of trade mark on the facts.

The Court of Appeal subsequently allowed an appeal brought by Arsenal against Laddie J's ruling, reversed his decision and applied the ECJ's preliminary ruling. The Court of Appeal was satisfied that the ECJ had stayed within its jurisdiction and that Laddie J had misinterpreted the ECJ's ruling. Nevertheless, the case serves to remind all concerned of the need for the national courts and the ECJ to maintain their respective jurisdictions (ECJ deals with interpretation of EC law; national courts decide questions of fact and apply law (as interpreted by the ECJ) to those facts).

Preliminary rulings as precedents

Preliminary rulings may also be cited as precedents in common law jurisdictions (*WH Smith, Do-It-All and Payless DIY Ltd v Peterborough CC* [1990]).

Is a preliminary ruling binding in subsequent cases? If the same issue arises again in a later case, then, under the doctrine of *acte clair*, there is no need to make a further reference. However, if the national court is unhappy with the previous ruling, it can make an additional reference, even if the matter is *acte clair* (*Costa v ENEL* [1964]). Indeed, a national court is obliged to either follow the ruling or make a new reference. This position is reflected in s 3(1) of the European Communities Act 1972.

REFORM

According to Rasmussen (2000) 37 CML Rev 1071, 'It is . . . a generally shared view today that the case for a comprehensive and profound judicial reform has become compelling.' Similarly, Johnston (2001) 38 CML Rev 499 states, 'Clearly, there is a serious workload problem for the Courts, due to a number of factors. . . . it is particularly serious in the context of references for a preliminary ruling . . .'.

There are several reasons for the 'workload problem':

■ The increasing number of Member States means more courts and tribunals, which means more referrals. In 2005, the ECJ gave rulings in 254 cases.

■ The increasing number of languages: in 2006 there are 27 States with 22 different languages. This has implications for *acte clair* as well as increasing the burden on the Court's translators.

■ The increasing scope and volume of EC legislation.

A solution was adopted in the Treaty of Nice, which came into effect in February 2003. For the first time, the CFI is allowed to deal with some requests for preliminary references. Article 225(3) of the EC Treaty (post-Nice) provides that the CFI shall have jurisdiction to give preliminary references 'in specific areas' to be laid down subsequently.

Article 225 goes on to provide:

> Where the CFI considers that the case requires a decision of principle likely to affect the unity or consistency of Community law, it may refer the case to the ECJ for a ruling. Decisions given by the CFI on questions referred for a preliminary ruling may exceptionally be subject to review by the ECJ . . . where there is a serious risk of the unity or consistency of Community law being affected.

There are potential problems with this new provision:

Interpretation. What does 'specific areas' involve? Other ambiguous words or phrases include 'decision of principle', 'likely to affect the unity or consistency', 'exceptionally', and 'serious risk'.

Procedure. Under the new procedure, when would the CFI be able to refer the case on? At the start of the case, or at any time? Some guidance may be sought from the procedure of the European Court of Human Rights.

It remains to be seen whether the Nice reform achieves the objective of reducing the ECJ's workload.

OTHER REFORM PROPOSALS

Note some other reforms that have been suggested in recent years. Arguments for and against are given below.

Restrict the right to seek references to national 'courts-of-last-resort' only

(For example the House of Lords.) This was proposed by the ECJ and CFI themselves in a consultation paper (1999). It was rejected by a special working group organised by the European Commission in 2000.

For: this would reduce the ECJ's workload by approximately 75 per cent.

Against: it threatens uniformity of EC law; threatens the dialogue that presently exists between ECJ and national courts; and would transfer problems to national systems, as parties would seek to keep appealing until they reached the court-of-last-resort.

Abolish the right of first-instance national courts and tribunals to seek references

This would affect county courts, magistrates' courts and most tribunals. The House of Lords, Court of Appeal, High Court (at least when acting as an appeal court), and certain tribunals (such as the Employment Appeal Tribunal and Immigration Appeal Tribunal) would all retain power to request references.

For: the ECJ's workload would be reduced by approximately 25 per cent.

Against: it threatens the uniformity of EC law; it could transfer problems to national systems, as parties would seek to appeal at least once.

'Case filtering'

The idea is that the ECJ should be allowed to select cases according to their novelty, complexity or importance.

For: this would obviously lead to a reduced ECJ workload; it might prompt national courts to be more selective; it would allow the ECJ to concentrate on those cases which are 'fundamental' to the uniformity and development of EC law.

Against: it threatens the uniformity of Community law; it could distort the judicial dialogue between the ECJ and national courts – the latter may not risk seeking a reference being rebuffed and therefore not send it.

Reword Art 234

In 1999, the European Commission proposed adding a sentence to the end of what is presently the second paragraph of the Article, requiring national courts to 'specify why the validity or interpretation of the rule of Community law raises difficulties in the case before it'. It was also proposed that the second and third paragraphs should be amended to impose a precondition that the question 'is of sufficient importance to Community law and that there is reasonable doubt as to the answer to that question'.

'Decentralisation'

This is perhaps the most radical reform, proposed by Jacques and Weiler (1990) 27 CML Rev 185, involving creating a series of regional courts to handle preliminary references. The ECJ would be installed at 'the apex of the system' and would be renamed 'European High Court of Justice' (EHCJ). National 'supreme' court references would go directly to the EHCJ. Below it would be four new 'Community Regional Courts' (CRCs) with 'jurisdiction to receive preliminary references from, and issue preliminary rulings to, national courts within each region'. They added, 'The legal status of the decision and rulings is a delicate matter'. They envisaged a hierarchical system with the EHCJ binding the CRCs. CRCs would be 'respectful' of each other but 'need not consider themselves strictly bound'.

For: a dramatically reduced workload for the ECJ; the CRCs could develop specialist expertise.

Against: there would be a risk of divergent rulings from the various CRCs.

You should now be confident that you would be able to tick all of the boxes on the checklist at the beginning of this chapter. To check your knowledge of Preliminary rulings why not visit the companion website and take the Multiple Choice Question test. Check your understanding of the terms and vocabulary used in this chapter with the flashcard glossary.

5

Free movement of workers

Understand what is meant by a worker and who constitutes a family member

Know the rights of residence of a worker and a family member

Understand the rights of a migrant worker and a family member under Regulation 1612/68 and be able to cite relevant cases

Understand the derogations based on public policy, public security and public health now stated in Directive 2004/38 which consolidates past case law on the derogations, and the procedural safeguards against expulsion

INTRODUCTION

Article 39 (formerly Art 48) of the EC Treaty provides for free movement of workers. Secondary legislation provides for detailed rules governing the right of entry into the territory of a Member State to carry out an economic activity, the right to remain in a Member State after having been employed there, and the right to equality of access to and conditions of employment on the same basis as nationals of the host State. These rights are subject to exceptions contained in the Treaty concerning public policy, public security and public health, and an exemption in the case of public service.

Initially, these rights were given to 'economically active' persons and their families, the purpose being to allow economically active persons the freedom to move around the Community so that 'workers' could move to jobs and higher wages in other parts of the Community. Free movement of workers helped to serve an economic objective and could not be regarded as an objective in itself.

Gradually, it has been recognised that the free movement of workers includes a social dimension. The Preamble to Regulation 1612/68 states that free movement is a 'fundamental right' of workers.

In 1990, freedom of movement was extended to three categories of persons who were not economically active – students, retired persons and persons of independent means. The Single European Act 1986 exhibited a greater awareness of the 'social dimension' to freedom of movement and it has now come to be regarded as an objective in its own right.

The Treaty on European Union establishes European citizenship, so that every person holding the nationality of a Member State is to be a citizen of the Union: Art 17. Every citizen of the Union will have the right to move and reside freely within the Territory of the Member States, subject to the limitations and conditions laid down by the Treaty and by measures adopted to give it effect (Art 18).

CITIZENSHIP

Nationality is tested by way of the national law of the State concerned. In the UK the relevant legislation is the British Nationality Act 1981 (as amended by the British Overseas Territories Act 2002). This point was confirmed in *Kaur* [2001]. K was born in Kenya in 1949. The British Nationality Act 1981 conferred on her the status of a 'British Overseas Citizen'. As such, she had, in the absence of special authorisation, no right under UK law to enter or remain in the UK. She challenged this, relying on the Citizenship provisions in the EC Treaty. The ECJ held that it was for each State to determine which persons qualified for nationality and, further, whether that automatically entitled them to rights of entry and residence. K therefore had no rights under Community law to challenge either her nationality status or the (lack of) rights conferred thereby under UK law.

The phrase 'national of a Member State' includes dual nationals. In *Micheletti* [1992], M, who was born in Argentina to Italian parents, had, according to Italian law, dual Argentine and Italian citizenship. After qualifying as a dentist in Argentina, he wished to set up a practice in Spain. However, the Spanish authorities rejected his application, as Spanish law deemed him to be Argentinean. The ECJ, however, held that as *Italian* law provided that he was an Italian national, there was no possibility of him being denied his rights under Community law because of *Spanish* law.

Article 18 is directly effective. In *Baumbast* [2002], the Court held: 'As regards, in particular, the right to reside within the territory of the Member States under Art 18, that right is conferred directly on every citizen of the Union by a clear and precise provision of the EC Treaty.' The Court did go on to qualify this statement in the next paragraph, where it stated that, 'Admittedly, that right for citizens of the Union to reside within the territory of another Member State is conferred subject to the limitations and conditions laid down by the EC Treaty and by the measures adopted to give it effect'.

> ### ▶ BAUMBAST (Case C-413/99)
>
> Mr Baumbast, a German national had left the UK although his child remained at school in the UK. Mrs Baumbast, a Colombian national, retained a right of residence in the UK as the child's 'primary carer'.

The decision to confer direct effect on Art 18 has produced some remarkable recent judgments. In *Zhu & Chen* [2004], the ECJ decided that an infant girl, born in Belfast in Northern Ireland to Chinese parents, had acquired Irish nationality and therefore EU citizenship. When her mother took the child to live in Cardiff in Wales, the Court accepted that EC law applied because the daughter was now a citizen of the EU resident in an EU state other than that of her nationality. (Even though the girl was born in Northern Ireland, part of the UK, Irish law confers Irish nationality on all persons born on the island of Ireland.) This gave the girl the right to reside anywhere in the UK. Finally, the girl's mother was entitled to reside with her in order to provide care for her (otherwise the girl's right of residence under Art 18 would have had extremely limited practical benefit).

More recently, in *Bidar* [2005], the ECJ decided that a French student attending university in the UK could invoke Art 18 by virtue of his status as an EU citizen resident in a state other than that of his nationality in order to acquire a right to claim a student loan.

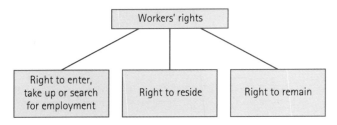

The Treaty of Amsterdam inserted a new title into the EC Treaty called 'visa, asylum, immigration and the free movement of persons'. This moves much of the old third pillar of the European Union into the EC Treaty itself. It also incorporates the Schengen Agreement and the Schengen Implementing Convention into EC law. The changes brought about by the Schengen Agreement include the abolition of border controls between participating States. The UK, Ireland and Denmark have opted out of most of the provisions of the Schengen Agreement.

An important directive came into effect on 30 April 2006. This is Directive 2004/38 which consolidates into a single directive all the Community secondary legislation concerning the right of entry and residence of EU citizens and their family members.

Briefly, under Art 6 of the directive, all EU citizens have an unconditional right of residence for up to three months in another Member State. After three months, the right of residence is conditional – Art 7. They will have the right of residence for more than three months if:

■ they are workers or self-employed; or

■ they have sufficient resources for themselves and their family so as not to be a burden on the social assistance system of the host Member State and they have comprehensive sickness insurance cover; or

■ they are enrolled on a course of study and have comprehensive sickness insurance cover; or

■ they are family members of the above.

Prior to enlargement on 1 May 2004 and 1 January 2007, Member States of the European Union expressed their fear of a massive arrival of workers from the new Member States. In response to these concerns, there are transitional arrangements regarding the sensitive issue of free movement of workers within the enlarged Union. The 15 Member States could allow total or partial freedom of movement for workers from the new Member States during this transitional period which may last up to a maximum of seven years from the date of accession. The following notes relate to free movement of workers as it applies to the 15 Member States (i.e. not to those states which **may** be subject to the transitional arrangements).

DEFINITION OF A 'WORKER'

The term 'worker' is not defined in the Treaty. It is a Community concept and is not derived from national law. Community legislation and case law make it clear that a 'worker' is an employed person, irrespective of whether he performs managerial or manual functions.

The ECJ has given a wide definition to the term 'worker'. In *Levin* [1982], a chambermaid, whose part time earnings fell below the Dutch minimum wage, supplemented these earnings with her own private income and had only taken the job to obtain the right to reside in the Netherlands. She was held to come within the Community definition of 'worker'.

▶ LEVIN (Case 53/81)

Mrs Levin was a British national working in Holland as a chambermaid for 20 hours per week. She was financially supported by her South African husband.

The ECJ held that she was a worker even though she had taken the job simply to qualify for worker status.

The applicant in *Levin* had not been a charge on the State and had supplemented her low level of earnings by her own private means. However, a person is still classified as a 'worker' if their earnings need to be augmented by supplementary benefit. In *Kempf* [1987], a German resident in the Netherlands who had to have his part time earnings boosted by supplementary benefit was still a 'worker'.

▶ KEMPF (Case 139/85)

A German music teacher who gave twelve lessons a week in the Netherlands was regarded as a worker for the purposes of Art 39 EC Treaty.

The definition of 'worker' has been extended to trainees (*Lawrie Blum* [1987]), where the applicant was a salaried trainee teacher who initially performed her duties under supervision but later independently came within the definition of 'worker'. The ECJ said that the test for a 'worker' was whether someone was in genuine and effective employment and performing services for an employer under his direction and control in return for remuneration.

In *Bernini* [1992], the ECJ said that in determining whether a trainee was in 'genuine and effective' employment, the national court may require proof that the trainee had worked long enough to become fully acquainted with the job performed.

The meaning of 'genuine and effective employment' was further considered in *Steymann* [1988]. A German national joined a Bhagwan community in the Netherlands. He was a qualified plumber and performed plumbing tasks for the community, and also carried out general domestic tasks and assisted in their commercial activities. He was not given formal wages but was given board, lodging and pocket money.

The ECJ considered whether the work was genuine and effective, and it was held that he was a worker even though he did not receive any direct remuneration. The benefits which the Community gave to its members were considered to be an indirect advantage for the work that was performed.

The employment must be a 'real' job. In *Bettray* [1989], Dutch legislation created 'social employment'. Jobs were specially created for people in order to support them, rehabilitate them or increase their capacity for normal work. This was done through State financed work associations, specially created for the purpose. Bettray was a German national living in Holland and was given 'social employment' as part of his treatment for drug addiction. He was receiving remuneration, but was not a 'worker', as the activities could not be regarded as genuine and effective. The job had been created to fit the applicant's capacity for work, as opposed to him being selected to do a particular job.

The ECJ continues to give judgments on the scope of the word 'worker', and maintains a flexible approach. In *Ninni-Orasche* [2003], the ECJ explicitly held that, although Ms Ninni-Orasche, an Italian national, had only worked for two and a half months (as a waitress) during a period of several years in Austria, she was not excluded from the scope of Article 39. The Court declined to impose any minimum thresholds in terms of time worked or money earned. Ultimately, whether or not she was a 'worker' was a question of fact for the national court, applying the 'genuine and effective' test. More recently, in *Trojani* [2004], the Court dealt with a case very similar to *Steymann*. This case involved a French national living in a Salvation Army hostel in Belgium, where he did various odd jobs for 'about 30 hours a week', in return for board and lodging and 'some pocket money', as part of a 'personal socio-occupational re-integration programme'. The Court refused to hold that, as a matter of law, *Trojani* did not satisfy the status of worker. Instead the Court offered the following summary of its case law to date:

> Neither the *sui generis* nature of the employment relationship under national law, nor the level of productivity of the person concerned, the origin of the funds from which the remuneration is paid or the limited amount of the remuneration can have any consequence in

regard to whether or not the person is a worker for the purposes of Community law.

SELF-EMPLOYED

Self-employed persons do not fall within the scope of the term 'worker'. However, this does not mean they are unprotected by EU law. Instead, the self-employed either fall under the scope of Art 43 EC (which deals with establishment) or Art 49 EC (the provision of services). Under Art 43, self-employed persons are allowed to travel to, reside in and set up a business in another EU Member State without discrimination. A good example is *Steinhauser* [1985], in which a self-employed German artist used Art 43 to establish the right to establish a business selling paintings in the French seaside resort of Biarritz under the same conditions as French nationals. Under Art 49, self-employed persons have the right to travel to other Member States on a temporary or periodic basis to provide services.

A good example is *Van Binsbergen* [1974], where a Dutch law requiring all lawyers who wished to appear in Dutch courts to be habitually resident in the Netherlands was held to be capable of breaching Art 49 as it restricted the freedom of lawyers resident in (say) Belgium from offering their legal services in the Netherlands.

THE WORKER'S FAMILY

Members of an immigrant worker's family have the right to reside in another Member State, even if they are not workers. The spouse and children of the worker can take up employment even if they are not EU nationals (*Gül* [1987]).

Directive 68/360 and Art 10 Regulation 1612 were repealed by Directive 2004/38, Art 2 of which defines a family member as

- The spouse of the worker.

- The partner with whom the Union citizen has contracted a registered partnership.

- The direct descendants of the worker who are under the age of 21 or who are dependants and those of the spouse or registered partner.

- The dependent direct relatives in the ascending line and those of the spouse or registered partner.

Under Art 7 of the Directive, family members may accompany or join the worker in the host state, i.e. they have the right of entry.

In addition, Art 3 of the Directive states that the host Member State shall facilitate entry for other persons, namely:

- Any other family members, irrespective of their nationality, who in the country from which they have come, are dependants or members of the household of the Union citizen having the primary right of residence (e.g. the worker) or where serious health grounds strictly require the personal care of the family member by the Union citizen.

The partner with whom he/she has a stable and duly attested relationship
The Member state will have to justify any denial of right of entry to the above.

It can be seen from the above that a cohabite of the worker will now have their entry to the host state facilitated. Compare the case of *Netherlands v Reed* [1986] argued under the old law.

In *Baumbast* [2002], the ECJ was asked whether the word 'descendants' meant the worker's children only, or whether it could be extended to include step-children. After the Advocate General pointed out that the key secondary legislation conferring rights on family members had been passed in the late 1960s, when the 'family unit' was much stronger than it is today, the Court decided to take a flexible view. G, a German national, had come to the UK to work with his Colombian wife and their daughter. There was a fourth member of the family: Mrs G's daughter from a previous relationship. The Court held that both daughters were entitled to residence in the UK as G's descendants.

Separated and divorced spouses
In *Diatta* [1985], the ECJ ruled that a separated spouse had the right to reside in the host Member State.

The situation could change if the parties actually divorced.

Directive 2004/38 deals with the question of right of residence for family members in the event of divorce, annulment of marriage or termination of a registered partnership.

FREE MOVEMENT OF WORKERS

In the case of EU family members, those events will not affect the family member's right of residence (Art 13(1)) but in the case of non-EU family members, retention of the right of residence is restricted, e.g. there will be no loss of the right of residence if, prior to divorce, the marriage had lasted at least three years, including one year in the host Member State.

Marriages of convenience

An important limitation was placed on the scope of the word 'spouse' in *Akrich* [2003]. The ECJ pointed out that only genuine marriages would be accepted. The Court stated that 'there would be an abuse if the facilities afforded by EC law in favour of migrant workers and their spouses were invoked in the context of marriages of convenience entered into in order to circumvent the provisions relating to entry and residence of nationals of non-Member States'.

Art 35 of Directive 2004/38 now specifically provides that Member States may adopt the necessary measures to refuse, terminate or withdraw any right conferred in the case of abuse of rights or fraud, such as marriages of convenience.

Dependant can be main breadwinner

In *Gül* [1987], a Cypriot doctor was married to a UK national and lived in Germany. He claimed that he was his wife's dependant, even though his wages were substantially in excess of hers. Nevertheless, he was held to be a dependant.

Children of workers

Children of workers are entitled not only to education but also to those rights which facilitate education, for example, rights to grants (*Casagrande* [1974]).

In *Echternach and Moritz* [1990], it was held that where a child returns to his State of origin with his parents after living and studying in another Member State, he may still be entitled to return to the host State without his parents and rely on Art 12, Regulation 1612/68 there, if educational institutions in his State of origin refuse to recognise qualifications obtained in the host State.

In *di Leo* [1990], the child of a migrant worker resident in Germany sought to return to her State of origin to undertake vocational training. There was a nationality requirement under German legislation for the award of financial assistance in respect of courses undertaken abroad.

The ECJ held that this nationality requirement was contrary to Art 12, Regulation 1612/68. Effective integration would be impeded if a migrant's family could not choose a course on the same basis as nationals of the host State.

Assistance under Art 12, Regulation 1612/68 is available even if the 'child' is 21 or over and is no longer financially dependent on his parents (*Gaal* [1995]). This is in contrast to Art 11, Regulation 1612/68. This Article gives the child of a 'worker' the right to take up employment in the host State but, for the purposes of these Articles, the child must be either under 21 or dependent on the worker.

MATERIAL SCOPE

Article 39(3) provides workers with the right to enter and remain in another Member State for the purpose of employment and also to remain in that Member State after the employment has finished. These rights are in outline and have been supplemented by secondary legislation.

THE RIGHT TO ENTER

This right has been granted by Regulation 1612/68 and has been widely interpreted by the ECJ to include the right to enter in search of work (*Procureur du Roi v Royer* [1976]).

Rights of residence up to three months

We have already noted that all EU citizens have a right of residence up to three months – Art 6(1) of Directive 2004/38. Under Art 6(2) non-EU family members enjoy the same rights as the EU citizen who they have accompanied or joined. However, they may be subject to a visa requirement under Regulation 539/ 2001. This right of residence of three months is subject to Art 14(1) of Directive 2004/38 ie 'as long as they do not become an unreasonable burden on the social assistance system of the host Member State'.

Rights of residence for more than three months

We have already seen that Art 7(1) of Directive 2004/38 provides that EU workers and their families have the right of residence for more than three months. This extends to non-EU family members of the worker under Art 7(2).

Although residence permits are abolished for EU citizens, Art 8 of the directive provides that Member States **may** require EU citizens to register with the competent authorities within a period of not less than three months from the date of arrival. A registration certificate will be issued immediately but in order for this to be issued, Member States may only require a valid identity card or passport and confirmation of engagement from an employer or a certificate of employment in the case of an EU worker.

Art 9 applies to non-EU family members who must apply for a residence card not less than three months from their date of arrival. This card is valid for five years. Art 10(2) sets out the documentation required before a card will be issued.

Rights of permanent residence
Art 16 of Directive 2004/38 indicates the conditions under which EU workers and their families may enjoy the right of permanent residence. Briefly, this right exists for EU workers and their families (including non-EU family members) if they have resided lawfully for a continuous period of five years in the host Member State.

Art 16(3) makes provision for temporary absences and Art 16(4) provides that the right of permanent residence may only be lost through absences of more than two consecutive years. Art 17 details the shorter qualifying period of residence for workers and their families where the worker has retired, or become incapacitated or died.

Rights of residence of work seekers
We have seen that all EU citizens have the right of residence for up to three months under Art 6 of Directive 2004/38. After three months, Art 14(4) provides that an expulsion measure cannot be taken against such persons if they entered the host Member State in order to seek employment if they can provide evidence that they are continuing to seek employment and that they have a genuine chance of being engaged.

ACCESS TO EMPLOYMENT/EQUALITY OF TREATMENT
There is a prohibition against discrimination on grounds of nationality laid down in general terms by Art 12 of the EC Treaty.

Regulation 1612/68 gives substance to the provisions of Art 12 and Art 39 of the EC Treaty. The Regulation is divided into three titles: Title I covering eligibility for employment, Title II concerning employment and equality of treatment and Title III which deals with families' rights (Arts 10 and 11 under this title have been repealed by Directive 2004/38).

Eligibility for employment (Arts 1–6 – Regulation 1612/68)

Any national of a Member State has the right to take up activity as an employed person and pursue such activity in the territory of another Member State, under the same conditions as nationals of that State: Art 1, Regulation 1612/68.

It is not possible to restrict the number or allocate a certain percentage of foreign workers to be employed in an activity or area of activity: Art 4, Regulation 1612/68.

States are entitled to permit the imposition on non-nationals of conditions 'relating to linguistic knowledge required by reason of the nature of the post to be filled': Art 3(1), Regulation 1612/68. In practice, this is one of the most important barriers to free movement. Workers are inhibited from moving to other States as they do not speak the language. Art 3(1) permits a requirement of linguistic knowledge where that is required for the post.

Language requirements can be imposed where there is an official policy to promote the language: *Groener v Minister for Education* [1989]. Teachers in Irish schools are required to be proficient in the Irish language. Under the Irish Constitution, Irish is the first official language of Ireland and national law had a clear policy of maintaining and promoting the Irish language. In *Groener*, the applicant was a Dutch woman who was barred from appointment as an art teacher at a college of marketing and design because she was unable to obtain the certificate. The Irish Government claimed that their action was justified on the basis of Art 3(1), Regulation 1612/68.

It was held that the EC Treaty does not prohibit the promotion by a Member State of its national language, provided that the measures taken to implement it are not disproportionate to the objective pursued and do not discriminate against the nationals of Member States. As teachers have a role in the promotion of Irish, a requirement that they have knowledge of Irish was reasonable provided it was applied in a non-discriminatory manner and the level of knowledge to be attained must not be excessive in relation to the objective pursued.

Equality of treatment (Arts 7–9 – Regulation 1612/68)

Article 7(1), Regulation 1612/68 provides that workers must be treated equally in respect of any conditions of employment and work, in particular remuneration, dismissal and, should a worker become unemployed, re-instatement or re-employment.

This covers both direct and indirect discrimination. In *Ugliola* [1969], a German employer took into account, for the purposes of seniority, employees' periods of national service in Germany. The applicant had done his national service in Italy and so it did not count. This was held to be discriminatory.

Social and tax advantages

Under Art 7(2), a migrant worker is entitled to the same 'social and tax advantages' as national workers.

The term 'social advantage' has been interpreted widely. In *Fiorini v SNCF* [1975], it was held to include a special rail reduction card to parents of large families, even though that is a benefit which does not attach to contracts of employment.

> ### ▶ FIORINI v SNCF (Case 32/75)
>
> The widow of a deceased Italian migrant worker, who was resident in France, was entitled to a fare reduction granted to families of French workers. The fare reduction was regarded as a social advantage which could not be interpreted restrictively.

A formula was developed for determining 'social or tax advantages' in *Ministère Public v Even* [1979]. Social or tax advantages are 'those which, whether or not linked to a contract of employment, are generally granted to national workers primarily because of their objective status as workers or by virtue of the mere fact of their residence on national territory'. An excellent example of Art 7(2) in practice is *Mutsch* [1985]. M was a German-speaking Luxembourg national resident in Belgium. He got into a fight with police and was subject to criminal proceedings. He claimed the right to have the case conducted in German. Belgian legislation provides that criminal proceedings may be heard in German if the accused so requests – but this right was available only to Belgian nationals. The ECJ held that Art 7(2) applied. Thus, the right to have a criminal prosecution conducted in German constituted a 'social and tax advantage'. It is important to note that M had this right only because Belgian nationals had the same right. Had he been working in the UK, for example, he would not have been able to insist on trial in German, because UK nationals have no such right either.

Social and tax advantages do, however, include benefits granted on a discretionary basis (*Reina* [1982]). An Italian couple were living in Germany. The husband was a 'worker' and they applied for a childbirth loan which was State-financed from the defendant bank. The loan was payable under German law to German nationals living in Germany. The bank argued that it was not a 'social advantage' under Art 7(2) as the loan had a political purpose: it was designed to increase the number of Germans. It was also a discretionary loan. It was also argued that the loan would be hard to recover from foreign nationals who returned home. The ECJ, applying the *Even* formula, held that the benefit granted on a discretionary basis was a social advantage.

Similarly, in *Castelli* [1984], an Italian, on being widowed, went to live with her son in Belgium. Applying the *Even* formula, it was held that she was entitled to claim a guaranteed income paid to all old people in Belgium. She had a right to reside with her son and so was entitled to the same social and tax advantages as Belgian workers and ex-workers.

> ### ▶ CASTELLI (Case 261/83)
>
> The Italian mother residing with her son, a migrant worker in Belgium, was entitled to the same social advantages as a Belgian family member.

It was held in *O'Flynn* [1996] that an allowance such as a funeral payment was within Art 7(2).

In *Baldinger* [2004], the ECJ decided that a war allowance paid by the Austrian government to former prisoners-of-war was not a 'social advantage', drawing attention to the fact that it was not 'linked to the status of worker'. This is, at first glance, difficult to reconcile with *Fiorini*, where the Court explicitly held that benefits need not be linked to any 'contract of employment'. Perhaps the answer is that the only possible claimants were Austrian nationals who had been taken as POWs during World War I and/or II, who would therefore be in their early 70s *at least*, which is above the normal retirement age.

In *Lebon* [1987], the ECJ held that a person who is seeking work, but has never worked, that is, a person in the *Antonissen* situation considered above, is not entitled to claim 'social and tax advantages'. However, this decision has recently been overruled. In *Collins* [2004], involving an dual Irish-American national seeking work in the UK who had been turned down for job-seekers' allowance, a social security benefit available to those looking for work in the UK, the ECJ held that his application should be considered and not automatically rejected. The Court invoked the introduction of EU citizenship in 1993 as justification for overruling *Lebon* on this point.

Vocational training

Article 7(3) entitles workers to access, under the same conditions as national workers, and to training in vocational schools and retraining centres.

The extent to which this provision applied to education was considered by the ECJ in *Brown* [1988] and *Lair* [1989]. Brown had obtained a place at Cambridge University to study engineering, and Lair had obtained a place at the University of Hanover to read languages. They claimed grants from the UK and German authorities respectively. Although Brown had dual French/British nationality, he and his family had been domiciled in France for many years. He obtained sponsorship from Ferranti and worked for them in Scotland for eight months, which was intended as a preparation for his university studies. Lair, a French national, had worked intermittently in Germany for five years with spells of involuntary unemployment. The authorities refused to give them grants.

▶ BROWN (Case 197/86)

Brown, a French national, obtained employment in Scotland which was described as pre-university industrial training.

The ECJ held that a national of another Member State will not be entitled to a grant for studies by virtue of his status as a worker

> where it is established that he acquired that status exclusively as a result of his being accepted for admission to university to undertake the studies in question.

▶ LAIR (Case 39/86)

Ms Lair, a French national living in Germany, was able to secure a grant for a place at Hanover University provided she could show that her course was connected in some way to her previous employment.

The refusal was challenged under, *inter alia*, Art 7(2) and Art 7(3), Regulation 1612/68.

The Court held that neither course constituted 'training in vocational schools' for the purpose of Art 7(3). The parties could succeed only under Art 7(2). The Court held that because Brown had acquired the status of a worker because of his acceptance into university, he could not rely upon Art 7(2). In Lair's case, the court drew a distinction purely between involuntary and voluntary unemployment. In the latter case, the applicant could claim a grant for a course only if there was a link between the studies and the previous work activity.

Art 7(3)(d) of Directive 2004/38 now specifically provides that a worker shall retain the status of worker if he/she embarks on vocational training. Unless he/she is involuntarily unemployed, the retention of the status of worker shall require the training to be related to the previous employment.

Brown was an attempt to plug a legal loophole whereby a student could acquire the status of 'worker' and could therefore claim all the financial benefits that flow from this under Art 7(2), Regulation 1612/68. In doing so, the ECJ has created a different category of 'worker' whereby a person can satisfy the definition of a worker under Art 48 (now Art 39) but may not qualify for all the rights which flow from this.

The importance of the ruling in *Brown* has diminished dramatically since the 1993 legislation conferring rights of residence on students – Directive 93/96. This was seen in *Grzelczyk* [2001]. G, a French national, was studying at university in Belgium. At the start of his final year, he applied for financial assistance, the minimex, from the Belgian social service to allow him to concentrate on his dissertation and practical training. This was refused on the basis that the minimex was payable only to Belgian nationals and migrant Community workers. The ECJ decided that, as a migrant student, G was protected by the directive. This alone did not entitle him to the minimex, but it did make him lawfully resident in Belgium. Moreover, this residency meant that the general prohibition on discrimination on grounds of nationality found in Art 12 of the EC Treaty applied and, hence, G was entitled to the minimex.

Trade union activities

Article 8, Regulation 1612/68 deals with discrimination in the area of trade union activities.

Workers from other Member States have a right to equal treatment as regards trade union membership and the rights that go with it, for example, the right to vote. They must be eligible for appointment to workers' representative bodies in the undertaking.

The provision was widely interpreted by the ECJ in *ASTI v Chambre des Employés Privés* [1991], and it now applies to all bodies whose primary function is the defence and representation of workers' interests.

However, immigrant workers may, under Art 8, be excluded from taking part in the management of bodies governed by public law and from holding an office governed by public law.

HOUSING

Article 9, Regulation 1612/68 gives immigrant Community workers the right to equal treatment with regard to housing, including public housing. This would bar any rule precluding them from putting their name down for, for example, council housing.

In *Commission v Greece* [1989], the ECJ held that national measures which restricted the right to own property in certain areas to Greek nationals were contrary to Art 9, Regulation 1612/68 and Art 39 of the EC Treaty.

INDIRECT DISCRIMINATION

Article 39 has been interpreted as prohibiting indirect as well as direct discrimination. However, indirect discrimination can be justified on objective grounds unrelated to nationality.

In cases of indirect discrimination, the ECJ has approached the question in three stages:

- Does the national measure come within the scope of the Treaty?

- Is the national provision discriminatory by working to the particular disadvantage of non-nationals?

- Is it objectively justified (subject to the principle of proportionality)?

In *Allué and Coonan* [1993], the applicants were foreign language assistants at the University of Venice. They were employed on renewable fixed term contracts. This type of contract is rare in Italy and the posts in question were designed for foreign nationals. They were held to be discriminatory. The ECJ held that the justifications put forward did not satisfy the principle of proportionality. There were less onerous ways of maintaining a staff-student ratio and ensuring that foreign language assistants maintained proficiency in their native tongues.

In *O'Flynn* [1996], a British regulation provided for a funeral payment. This was a means tested social benefit and was payable to cover the costs incurred by the claimant or a member of his family on the occasion of a death in the family. It was payable only if the funeral or cremation took place within the UK. The applicant was an Irish former migrant worker whose application for a payment for his son's funeral was refused on the grounds that the burial did not take place in the UK.

It was held to be indirectly discriminatory, and consequently had to be objectively justified, subject to the principle of proportionality. The objective behind the payment was the protection of public health, and this objective should be sought even if the funeral took place outside of the UK. Purported justifications based on the cost and practical difficulties of paying the allowance were also rejected. The cost of transporting the coffin to a place distant from the deceased's home was not covered by the payment. The allowance could be fixed by reference to the cost of a reasonable burial in the UK.

The ECJ also said that it was not necessary to show that the provision actually affected a substantially higher proportion of migrant workers: it was sufficient that it was likely to have such an effect.

PRIVATE COLLECTIVE EMPLOYMENT RULES

Although Art 39 of the EC Treaty is addressed to Member States, it was held in the case of *Walrave and Koch v Association Union Cycliste Internationale* [1974] that it was of horizontal, as well as vertical, direct effect. The case involved the rules of a sporting association which required the pacemaker of a cycling team to be of the same nationality as the other members of the team. The association was not a public or State body. It was held that Art 39 applies, even to rules of private bodies, in respect of rules which collectively regulate employment. Sport is subject to Community law insofar as it constitutes an 'economic activity'.

In *Union Royale Belge des Sociétés de Football Association ASBL v Bosman* [1996], it was held that Art 39 precluded the application of rules of sporting associations whereby a professional footballer could not, on the expiry of his contract, be employed by a club in another Member State unless a transfer fee was paid to the former club. It also prohibited the rules of the European football confederation (UEFA) which limited the number of professional players from another EC country that a team could field.

The ECJ rejected the objective justifications that had been put forward. It had been argued that transfer fees maintain a balance between large and small clubs. The ECJ felt that the system patently did not achieve this aim, as the richest clubs were able to obtain the services of the best players and the existence of financial resources was a decisive factor in the sport. The second purported justification was also rejected. This argument claimed that transfer fees gave clubs an incentive to train and develop talent. The presence of talent could not be predicted with certainty and only a limited number of players went on to play professionally.

In *Lehtonen v Fédération Royale Belge des Sociétés de Basket-ball* [2000] a Finnish basketball player was transferred to a Belgian club after the completion of the 1995–96 Finnish championship. The player was fielded during the later stages of the Belgian championship of the same year. The Belgian club was penalised as the transfer had taken place after the FIBA deadline for transfers of players within the European zone (there were different deadlines for international transfers). The deadline was justified by FIBA as a means of preventing undue disruption of national championships by late transfers. The court ruled that this type of deadline could possibly be justified on the grounds of public interest, but that the deadlines for European transfers and non-member transfers would have to be the same.

Surprisingly, it is only relatively recently that the Court has been asked to decide whether Art 39 has 'full' horizontal direct effect; that is, whether it can be relied upon against a private employer. In *Angonese* [2000], the Court held that it can. When A, an Italian national, applied for a job with a bank in the Italian city of Bolzano he was unsuccessful because one of the conditions of entry was possession of a special certificate (issued only by the local authorities) confirming bilingualism in German and Italian. A, who had studied languages at the University of Vienna, contended that his degree certificate should be acceptable and refusal to accept it would constitute indirect discrimination contrary to Art 39. The ECJ agreed.

EXCEPTIONS

Article 39(3) allows an exception from the free movement of workers provisions where it is justified on grounds of public policy, public security or public health.

Art 39(3) is further fleshed out by Directive 2004/38 which repeals Directive 64/221 and incorporates much of the former case law which is therefore considered below.

MEANING OF 'PUBLIC POLICY'

In *Van Duyn v Home Office* [1974], it was said that the concept of public policy is subject to control by Community institutions but that the definition of public policy can vary from State to State.

In *Rutili v French Minister of the Interior* [1975], it was held that for the public policy exception to be invoked, the threat must be genuine and serious. Restrictions are subject to the proportionality principle.

In *R v Bouchereau* [1977], the test was expressed as: '... a genuine and sufficiently serious threat to the requirements of public policy affecting one of the fundamental principles of society.'

MEANING OF 'PUBLIC SECURITY'

This is reserved for serious crimes and subversive, anti-State activities, eg terrorism or espionage. Public security was specifically referred to in *Otieza Olazabal* [2002], involving a member of ETA (*Euskadi Ta Askatasuna* (Basque Homeland and Freedom)). The case involved a Spanish national threatened with deportation from France following conviction of terrorism offences. The ECJ dealt with it as a case of 'public security', stating:

> The defendant in the main proceedings ... has been sentenced in France to 18 months' imprisonment and a four-year ban on residence for conspiracy to disturb public order by intimidation or terror ... he formed part of an armed and organised group whose activity constitutes a threat to public order in French territory. Prevention of such activity may, moreover, be regarded as falling within the maintenance of public security.

Personal conduct and criminal convictions

Art 27(2) of Directive 2004/38 states that 'measures taken on grounds of public policy or public security shall comply with the principle of proportionality and shall be based exclusively on the personal conduct of the individual concerned'.

It continues that previous criminal convictions shall not in themselves constitute grounds for taking such measures. The personal conduct of the individual concerned must represent a genuine, present and sufficiently serious threat affecting one of the fundamental interests of society.

Art 27(1) states that 'the grounds shall not be invoked to serve economic ends'.

Cases on the meaning of personal conduct and the effect of criminal convictions

In *Van Duyn v Home Office* [1974], it was held that present association with a group or organisation could count towards personal conduct, but that past association could never do so.

Van Duyn was a Dutch national, who was refused entry into the UK on grounds of public policy. She wished to take up employment with the Church of Scientology. Scientology was not illegal but was considered socially undesirable by the UK Government. The refusal was based on personal conduct due to the applicant's association with the Scientology sect. The case was the first preliminary reference made by a court of the UK, and the controversial result has been explained as an attempt by the ECJ to be accommodating to the UK on its first reference.

The ECJ held that conduct does not have to be illegal to justify exclusion but must be socially harmful, and administrative measures must have been taken to counteract activities.

▶ VAN DUYN v HOME OFFICE (Case 41/74)

Ms Van Duyn was a Dutch national and a member of the Church of Scientology. She was refused entry to work for the College of Scientology in the UK.

The ECJ held that present membership of an organisation, against which administrative measures had been taken, did constitute personal conduct for the purposes of Art 39(3).

The ECJ has, after *Van Duyn*, laid down much stricter tests. In *R v Bouchereau* [1977], a French national, resident in the UK, who had twice been convicted of drugs offences, was threatened with deportation from the UK. It was held that previous convictions should only be taken into account if there was a present threat to requirements of public policy, but past conduct alone could constitute a threat if it was sufficiently grave.

▶ R v BOUCHEREAU (Case 30/77)

Bouchereau, a French citizen, working in the UK, was given a suspended sentence for a drug offence.

The ECJ held that measures to deport him could only be taken if he posed a genuine and serious threat to society.

In *Adoui and Cornuaille* [1982], two French waitresses were working in a bar in Belgium but were also working as prostitutes. Prostitution was legal in Belgium but was discouraged. The Belgian authorities denied them a residence permit.

It was held that Member States could not deny residence to non-nationals because of conduct which, when attributable to a State's own nationals, did not give rise to repressive measures or other genuine and effective measures to combat such conduct.

> ### ▶ ADOUI and CORNUAILLE v BELGIUM (Case 115/81)
>
> French prostitutes could not be denied entry to Belgium where prostitution was not illegal.

The correctness of the decision in *Adoui and Cornuaille* was confirmed in *Jany and Others* [2001]. The case concerned a number of female prostitutes from the Czech Republic who were working in Amsterdam. They successfully resisted deportation on the basis that the Dutch authorities' attitude to similar activities on the part of their own nationals did not attract repressive measures.

In *Bonsignore* [1975], an Italian living in Germany was threatened with deportation after conviction of a criminal offence as a deterrent. It was held that a deportation order can be made only in connection with breaches of peace and public security which may be committed by the individual concerned.

Similar issues arose in *Calfa* [1999]. C, an Italian national, was convicted for possession and use of prohibited drugs whilst in Greece. A Greek court expelled her for life from Greece, as required by Greek law. C appealed against the expulsion, arguing that Greece was not empowered to expel a national of another Member State for life if a comparable measure could not be taken against a Greek citizen. The ECJ agreed: automatic expulsion (without any account being taken of the personal conduct of the offender or of the danger that that person represented) was contrary to the 'personal conduct' requirement in Art 3(1) of Directive 64/221.

The latest decision on 'personal conduct' is that in *Orfanopoulos* [2004], involving provisions of German law very similar to that in *Calfa*, providing for automatic deportation of foreign nationals convicted of certain drugs and public order offences. The ECJ held that:

'Community law precludes the deportation of a national of a Member State ... *where such measure automatically follows a criminal conviction*, without any account being taken of the personal conduct of the offender or of the danger which that person represents for the requirements of public policy.'

PROTECTION AGAINST EXPULSION

Art 28 Directive 2004/38 provides that before taking an expulsion decision on grounds of public policy or public security, the host Member State shall take account of considerations such as how long the individual concerned has resided on its territory, his/her age, state of health, family and economic situation, social and cultural integration into the host Member State and the extent of his/her links with the country of origin.

Even under the former law, the significance of the individual having a family in the host Member State was taken into account.

Significance of the individual having a family

In *Orfanopoulos* [2004], a Greek national had married a German woman and they had three children. He was a repeat drugs offender who had spent several years in and out of German prisons and drug rehabilitation clinics before eventually facing deportation. The ECJ was asked what significance, if any, his factual situation had on the German authorities' entitlement to pursue deportation. The Court decided (having made reference to the right to respect for a family life, protected by Article 8 of the European Convention of Human Rights) that it was a relevant factor:

'It is clear that the removal of a person from the country where close members of his family are living may amount to an infringement of the right to respect for family life ... account must be taken, particularly, of the nature and seriousness of the offences committed by the person concerned, the length of his residence in the host Member State, the period which has elapsed since the commission of the offence, the family circumstances of the person concerned and the seriousness of the difficulties which the spouse and any of their children risk facing in the country of origin of the person concerned.'

This does not, of course, say that an individual who happens to be married to a national of the host State cannot be deported; but it does say that a person is entitled to have his or her 'family circumstances' taken into account.

PUBLIC HEALTH

Under Art 29(1) of Directive 2004/38, the only diseases which can justify restricting the right of entry and residence on the ground of public health are those with epidemic potential as defined by the World Health Organisation and other infectious diseases or other contagious parasitic diseases if they are subject to protection provisions applying to nationals of the host Member State.

PROCEDURAL PROTECTION

This is now contained in Articles 30–33 of Directive 2004/38. Briefly Art 30 is concerned with notification of decisions and requires the persons concerned to be notified in writing of any decision taken under Art 27(1) above. They are required to be informed precisely and in full of the public policy, public security or public health grounds on which the decision in their case is based, unless this is contrary to the interests of State security. The notification must also specify the court or administrative body to which they may appeal. Except in cases of urgency, the time allowed to leave the host Member State shall be not less than one month from the date of notification.

Art 31 provides procedural safeguards and gives detail of access to judicial and administrative redress procedures in the host Member State. Art 32 deals with the duration of exclusion orders and Art 33 stipulates that expulsion orders may not be issued by the host Member State as a penalty other than in circumstances which fulfil the conditions set out in Arts 27–29.

PUBLIC SERVICE EXEMPTION

Free movement of workers does not apply to public service under Art 39(4). This could be a very significant exemption, but has been interpreted narrowly.

In *Commission v Belgium (Re Public Employees)* [1979], all posts in the 'public service' were limited to Belgian nationals. The Belgian Government argued that those jobs were within the public service. The ECJ held that it only applied to the exercise of official authority and to employees who were safeguarding the general interests of the State.

> ▶ **COMMISSION v BELGIUM (Re Public Employees)**
> **Case 149/79)**
>
> Belgian law reserved posts in the public service for Belgian nationals only.

> The ECJ ruled that the public service exception applied only to posts which involved 'direct or indirect participation in the exercise of powers conferred by public law and duties designed to safeguard the general interests of the state'.

Where the 'public service' derogation does apply, then Member States are free to exclude foreign nationals altogether. In *Anker v Germany* [2003], the ECJ held that provisions of German law restricting the position of ship's master to German nationals was justifiable in principle on the basis that ships' masters had responsibility for maintaining public order on the ship; they also had powers in respect of marriages and deaths occurring on board. The ECJ did qualify its judgment by holding that:

> The scope of [Art 39(4)] must be limited to what is strictly necessary for safeguarding the general interests of the Member State concerned, which cannot be imperilled if rights under powers conferred by public law are exercised only sporadically, even exceptionally, by nationals of other Member States.

Other occupations where the derogation may apply would seem to be the security services (in the UK, that is MI5 and MI6), the armed forces, the higher echelons of the civil service, the police force, and so on. Indeed, in the UK, membership of the British Army's fighting units is restricted to British, Irish and Commonwealth nationals.

The wholly internal rule

A national of a Member State who has never exercised the right of freedom of movement within the EC is unable to rely on Art 39. The leading case is *R v Saunders* [1979], involving a woman from Northern Ireland who was convicted of theft at Bristol Crown Court and bound over on condition that she returned to Northern Ireland and did not return to England or Wales for three years. However, within six months she was arrested in Wales. She claimed that this breached Art 39, but the ECJ disagreed. All the facts were 'internal' to the UK, so Community law did not apply.

However, there is an important exception to this rule: returnees. People who have left one Member State to work or study abroad can rely on Art 39 on their return. This could allow them to invoke Community law to have qualifications awarded abroad recognised at home (*Bouchoucha* [1990]; *Kraus* [1993]; *Fernández de Bobadilla* [1999]; *D'Hoop* [2002]).

You should now be confident that you would be able to tick all of the boxes on the checklist at the beginning of this chapter. To check your knowledge of Free movement of workers why not visit the companion website and take the Multiple Choice Question test. Check your understanding of the terms and vocabulary used in this chapter with the flashcard glossary.

6

EC sex equality legislation

Recognise the scope of Art 141 of the EC Treaty ☐

Understand the provisions of the Equal Treatment Directive
2006/54 in relation to equal pay and equal treatment ☐

Give examples of the rulings of the ECJ in cases on equal pay
and equal treatment ☐

FREEDOM FROM DISCRIMINATION

From the outset, it is important to distinguish between direct discrimination and indirect discrimination. These concepts are both defined in the new Equal Treatment Directive 2006/54. Direct discrimination is where one person is treated less favourably on grounds of sex than another is, has been, or would be treated in a comparable situation. Indirect discrimination is where an apparently neutral provision, criterion or practice would put persons of one sex at a particular disadvantage compared with persons of the other sex, unless that provision, etc is objectively justified by a legitimate aim, and the means of achieving that aim are appropriate and necessary.

The new directive also provides that discrimination includes harassment and sexual harassment, as well as any less favourable treatment based on a person's rejection of or submission to such conduct and any instruction to discriminate against persons on grounds of sex.

The new Equal Treatment Directive 2006/54 is a consolidating directive, replacing the Equal Pay Directive 75/117 and the Equal Treatment Directive 76/207. The new directive incorporates many rulings of the ECJ and therefore much former case law is included below. It does not introduce any substantially new amendments.

Briefly therefore it governs:

- equal treatment in access to employment and promotion;

- vocational training;

- working conditions including pay;

- occupational social security.

EQUAL PAY – THE LEGISLATIVE FRAMEWORK

Art 141 of the EC Treaty provides that each Member State shall ensure that the principle of equal pay for male and female workers for equal work or work of equal value is applied.

The Equal Pay Directive 75/117 which fleshed out the provisions of Art 141 has now been repealed and replaced by Directive 2006/54 which incorporates much of the former case law on pay.

ARTICLE 141

Direct effect of Art 141

Art 141 which established the principle of equal pay for men and women has direct effect, ie it creates rights and obligations for individuals which may be enforced in national courts.

In *Defrenne v SABENA (No 2)* [1976], the European Court of Justice (ECJ) held that Art 119 (now Art 141) had horizontal and vertical direct effect.

In the interests of legal certainty, the effect of the judgment was limited, so that claims for backdated pay could only be made from the date of judgment, unless a claim had already been brought.

What is 'pay' for the purposes of Art 141?

Pay is defined as the 'ordinary basic minimum wage or salary' plus 'any other consideration', whether in cash or in kind, for which the worker receives directly or indirectly in respect of his employment from his employer (Article 141(2) EC).

State pension schemes

In *Defrenne v Belgium (No 1)* [1971] the ECJ ruled that social security schemes or benefits, in particular retirement pensions, directly governed by legislation without any element within the undertaking which apply to general categories of workers fall outside the meaning of 'pay' for the purposes of Art 141.

Criticisms of *Defrenne (No 1)* test:

- ▦ it discriminates between employees whose employers operate one form of pension scheme rather than another;

- ▦ the operation of Art 141 may be dependent on the national organisation of pension schemes.

The first of a number of exceptions to *Defrenne (No 1)* was laid down in *Liefting* [1984]. Contributions to a State social security scheme affected the level of gross pay, and therefore the level of other benefits did constitute 'pay' for the purpose of Art 141.

Article 141 was again held to be applicable to a statutory social security benefit in *Rinner-Kühn* [1989]. In this case, statutory sick pay in the form of wages which an employer was required to pay by law in the event of illness was held to be 'pay'. The employer was required to continue paying an employee who was incapable of working for a period of up to six weeks. Thereafter, the social security system paid 80 per cent of the normal earnings of a worker. The case is hard to distinguish from *Defrenne (No 1)* and yet the opposite conclusion was reached. This has created uncertainty as to the true state of the law. National legislation which allowed employers to maintain a global difference between two categories of worker, part time and full time, was contrary to Art 141. It also fell within 141 as it arose from the employment relationship. As part time workers were predominantly female, it constituted indirect discrimination and had to be objectively justified.

Occupational pensions

A further area of difficulty has been occupational pension schemes. Many occupational pension schemes operate in addition to a State scheme, have some State support and in some cases are organised by the State.

Directive 86/378 on the implementation of the principle of equal treatment for men and women in occupational social security schemes showed that the Council considered occupational pensions to be more a matter of social security rather than pay.

However, the ECJ took a different view in *Bilka-Kaufhaus v Karin Weber von Hartz* [1986] in which it held that an occupational pension entirely financed by the employer was within Art 141. The scheme was adopted in accordance with German legislation applicable to such pension schemes but it had been set up voluntarily through the agreement between Bilka and the staff committee representing its employees. It was a contractual rather than a statutory scheme and was financed entirely by the employer. This led the ECJ to hold that the pension was capable of constituting 'pay' under Art 141.

This interpretation has clearly affected the relationship between Art 141 and Directive 86/378. By concluding that Art 141 could apply to occupational social security schemes, the Directive is largely redundant and is of use only in relation to indirect discrimination. This re-ordering of the frontier between Art 141 and the secondary legislation relating to equality has advantages for applicants, as Art 141 has both vertical and horizontal direct effect.

The way in which pensions were organised in the UK has caused particular difficulties with regard to Art 141. The UK provided for an additional State pension in addition to the basic retirement pension in the form of a State Earnings Related Pension Scheme (SERPS). This allowed for a supplementary State pension related to earnings in addition to the basic pension. However, the cost of the scheme proved to be prohibitive and the Government sought to privatise this supplemental pension in the form of 'contracting out'.

The issue then arose as to whether these 'contracted out' pensions were within or outside Art 141. The answer came in *Barber v Guardian Royal Exchange Assurance Group* [1990]. Barber was an employee of the defendants and was made redundant at the age of 52. His occupational pension was a contracted out scheme and he claimed that it was in breach of Art 141. A woman would have been entitled to an immediate pension at the age of 50, whereas a man had to wait until 55 before receiving his pension. Barber had suffered a detriment by waiting longer for his pension on grounds of his sex. In addition, the statutory redundancy scheme which was also payable at different ages for men and women was challenged.

The ECJ held that Art 141 applied to contracted out occupational pension schemes and to all redundancy payments. The ECJ pointed out that the pension scheme in *Defrenne (No 1)* had been determined less by the employment relationship than by considerations of social policy. Art 141 cannot encompass social security schemes or benefits, directly governed by legislation without any element of agreement within the undertaking or occupational branch concerned, which are compulsorily applicable to general categories of worker. By contrast, contracted out schemes are the result either of an agreement between the workers or employers or of a unilateral decision of the employer. They are wholly financed by the employer or by both the employer and employees, without any contribution by the public authorities in any circumstances.

Contracted out schemes are not applicable to general categories of worker but apply to workers employed by certain undertakings. Although such schemes are established in conformity with national legislation, they are governed by their own rules.

The ECJ recognised that the judgment in *Barber* might cause confusion, not least because of the existence of Art 9, Directive 86/378. *Barber* illustrates how the ECJ has moved the frontiers between Art 141 and secondary legislation.

There were also misgivings about the cost of implementing the judgment. It was thought to be particularly expensive in the Netherlands and the UK because of the way in which their pensions industries were organised. The UK pensions industry warned that it would cost £50 billion to implement.

As a result, the ECJ placed a temporal limitation on *Barber* that the judgment could not be applied retrospectively. Consequently, with the exception of actions already pending, no claim could be brought for pension benefits for the period before the date of judgment on 17 May 1990. Although the justification for this temporal limitation was based on legal certainty, it was also influenced by costs considerations.

This temporal limitation caused considerable confusion. Did it mean that contributions payable after 17 May 1990 had to be equal or did it mean that the benefits received after that date had to be equal? If it meant the latter, then contributions made on an unequal basis before 17 May 1990 would have to be equalised. The Member States sought to restrict the temporal effects of the *Barber* judgment in a Protocol to the Treaty on European Union:

> ... benefits under occupational pension schemes shall not be considered as remuneration if and in so far as they are attributable to periods of employment prior to 17 May 1990.

This has led to further criticism that the Member States were using their legislative function to usurp the interpretative function of the ECJ. A crisis between the institutions of the Community was averted by the case of *Ten Oever* [1993]. Equality of treatment may be claimed only in relation to benefits payable in respect of periods of employment subsequent to 17 May 1990. It was also held that benefits paid to an employee's survivor were within Art 119 (now Art 141), since the benefit was paid by reason of the employment relationship. The case of *Newstead* would now appear to be weak authority.

Further clarification of the *Barber* judgment was obtained in *Coloroll Pension Trustees Ltd v Russell* [1994]. It was held that Art 141 applied to pensions paid under a trust, even though pension fund trustees are not parties to the employment relationship. Trustees are still under this obligation to observe Art 141, even if this is contrary to the trust deed. The equal treatment principle also applies to employers who have transferred their acquired rights from another pension fund which has not observed Art 141. This means that pension fund trustees may have to make good the cost of another company failing to comply with Art 141.

The case of *Beune* [1994] again raised the issue of whether a pension was within Art 141 as a result of being part of the employment relationship, or whether it was part of social policy and therefore governed by Directive 79/7. This involved civil service pensions, and the ECJ held that, even where a pension was affected by 'considerations of social policy, of State organisation, or of the ethics or even of budgetary considerations' which could point to being classed as social security, it could still be classed as pay and consequently come within Art 141, even though the pension is paid by a public employer, so long as:

■ it concerned a particular category of worker rather than general categories;

■ it was directly related to the period of service;

■ its amount was calculated by reference to the employee's last salary.

The case of *Neath v Hugh Steeper Ltd* [1993] revolved around a 'defined benefit' scheme. In such a scheme, the criteria for the pension are fixed in advance and are fixed as a fraction of the final year's salary for each year of service. Employee contributions must be the same for men and women. However, employer contributions can vary over time. This was the result of using sex based actuarial factors, as the pensions actually paid would vary. Statistically, women live longer than men, and hence the pension is needed for a longer period. A number of objections can be made to this. First, it treats individual employees on the basis of stereotypical assumptions. Secondly, a man could receive less in the event of a capital sum on redundancy, transfer benefits or a deferred pension. The ECJ held that the employer contributions were not 'pay' within the meaning of Art 141. The contributions were made to ensure an adequate pension.

In *Roberts v Birds Eye Walls Ltd* [1993], Mrs Roberts was forced to retire early on grounds of ill health. She received a bridging pension as part of an occupational pension scheme. The payment was made *ex gratia* and its aim was to place employees in the same financial position they would have been in if they had not been forced to take early retirement. Women received the State pension aged 60, whereas men had to wait until the age of 65. The bridging pension paid to women between the ages of 60 and 65 was lower than that for men, as the employers took into account the State pension. Women consequently needed less to bring them up to the financial position they were in whilst working.

The ECJ found that the purpose of the bridging pension was to maintain the level of income. Consequently, the ECJ did not find the decision discriminatory. This decision was recently confirmed in *Hlozek* [2004], another case involving bridging pensions.

To conclude, having broadened the concept of 'pay' in *Barber*, the ECJ drew back in *Neath* and other post-*Barber* cases. The outcome of these post-*Barber* cases with all their anomalies is now contained in Title II – Chapter 2 of the new consolidating Equal Treatment Directive 2006/54.

Other examples of what constitutes pay

In *Gillespie v Northern Health and Social Services Board* [1996], the applicants' maternity pay was calculated by reference to the last two pay cheques prior to taking maternity leave. They received full pay for four weeks, nine-tenths of full weekly pay for a further two weeks thereafter, and then half pay for 12 weeks. Whilst on maternity leave, a pay rise was awarded which was backdated, but the applicants did not receive the benefit of this pay rise. The applicants claimed discrimination, first, on the grounds that their pay had been reduced during maternity leave and, secondly, on grounds that they had not received the benefit of the backdated pay rise. It was held that neither Art 141 nor the Equal Pay Directive (75/117 (see below)) required the women to receive full pay during their maternity leave, provided that the amount was not so low as to jeopardise the purpose of maternity leave. However, the applicants were entitled to pay rises awarded between the start of the payment of maternity pay and the end of maternity leave.

The Alabaster case

Gillespie was followed in *Alabaster v Woolwich Building Society* [2004], a case which attracted considerable publicity at the time. Ms Alabaster worked for the Woolwich between December 1987 and August 1996. In January 1996 she went on maternity leave. In December 1995, she had been awarded a pay rise, but her maternity pay was calculated on the basis of her salary in October 1995. The pay-rise was not back-dated. Ms Alabaster argued that the failure to take account of her salary increase was contrary to Art 141. The ECJ agreed: had she not gone on maternity leave, she would have received the full benefit of the pay rise throughout her period of maternity leave. Therefore, to refuse to acknowledge the pay rise in calculating maternity pay constituted a breach of Article 141.

This case law is now reflected in Article 15 of the new Directive 2006/54 which provides that a woman on maternity leave shall be entitled, after the end of her period of maternity leave, to return to her job or to an equivalent post on terms and conditions which are no less favourable to her and to benefit from any improvement in working conditions to which she would have been entitled during her absence.

Article 141 does not apply to working conditions

In *Defrenne v SABENA (No 3)* [1979], it was held that Art 141 does not stretch to equality of working conditions other than pay between men and women. Consequently, an attempt to use Art 141 as a means of ensuring equality of retirement ages under Art 141 failed.

Similarly, in *Burton v British Railways Board* [1982], access to a voluntary early retirement redundancy scheme, where women could apply earlier than men, was governed by the Equal Treatment Directive and not by Art 141.

'Pay' includes non-contractual benefits

Benefits need only be granted in respect of employment to come within Art 141 and do not have to arise from a contractual relationship: *Garland v British Rail Engineering Ltd* [1982]. Special travel facilities provided to retired male workers and their families which are not available to retired female employees and their families are 'pay' within Art 141.

Transparency and the burden of proof

In the case of *Enderby v Frenchay HA* [1993], the claimant was a speech therapist and her profession was overwhelmingly dominated by females. She claimed that members of her profession were discriminated against by being paid less well than clinical psychologists and pharmacists. The work performed by these professions were of equal value to hers, and consisted mainly of men. The ECJ held that normally the person alleging discrimination, that is, the worker, must prove it, but where a *prima facie* case of discrimination exists it is for the *employer* to show that there are objective reasons for the difference in pay. The fact that the difference has been caused by separate collective bargaining processes cannot be sufficient objective justification. It was for the national court to determine whether difficulties in recruitment constituted objective justification.

A similar conclusion was also reached in *Handels- og Kontorfunktionaerernes Forbund i Danmark v Dansk Arbejdsgiverforening ex p Danfoss* [1989]. Danfoss had paid the same basic wage to employees in the same group, but it also awarded individual pay supplements which were calculated on the basis of mobility, training and seniority. These criteria were likely to disadvantage women, as they tended to have greater restrictions on their mobility and less seniority due to domestic caring duties for which they were still disproportionately responsible. The case had been brought by two female employees who had received 7 per cent less pay than male workers in the same wage group. The ECJ held that, where an undertaking applies a system of pay that is lacking in transparency, it is for the employer to show that the wages system is not discriminatory if a female worker establishes a *prima facie* case by showing that, in relation to a large number of employees, the average pay for women is less than men.

Transparency was also an issue in the *Royal Copenhagen* case [1995]. The complaint was that Royal Copenhagen's blue pattern painters, who were predominantly women, were paid less than automatic machine operators, who were exclusively men. The pay consisted of a fixed element and a variable element. The fixed element was not the same for the different groups of workers but the union asserted that the different work was of equal value. The variable element consisted of piece work which varied according to the output of each individual worker. It was held that Art 119 (now Art 141) applied to these piece work pay schemes. The mere finding that in a piece work pay scheme the average pay of a group of workers consisting mainly of women was appreciably lower than the average pay of a group of workers consisting predominantly of men carrying out work to which equal value was attributed was not sufficient to establish discrimination with regard to 'pay'.

However, where it was not possible to identify the factors determining the variable elements, the employer might have to bear the burden of proving that the differences in pay were not due to discrimination. Otherwise, the workers might be deprived of any effective means of enforcing the principle of equal pay. The pay differential would not constitute discrimination if it could be objectively justified.

In comparing the average pay of the two groups, the groups chosen had to comprise a relatively large number of workers so as to ensure that differences in pay were not due to fortuitous or short term factors or to differences in workers' individual output.

The ECJ restated the principle that there should be equal pay where the elements of pay were determined by collective bargaining. However, the national court could take into account whether the differences in pay were objectively justified.

Note that Art 19 of the new Equal Treatment Directive 2006/54 specifically requires Member States to ensure that, where an employee establishes facts from which it may be presumed that there has been direct or indirect discrimination, it is for the respondent employer to prove that there has been no breach of the principle of equal treatment.

PART TIME WORKERS

The cases relating to part time workers have developed the law relating to indirect discrimination. Provisions which treat part time workers adversely are not *prima facie* discriminatory, as they affect both sexes. However, as part time workers are predominantly women, such provisions will have a greater adverse impact on them.

In *Jenkins v Kingsgate (Clothing Productions) Ltd* [1981], it was held that a variation in pay between full time and part time workers does not breach Art 141, provided the hourly rates are applied without distinction based on sex, and differences are 'objectively justified'. This imported the concept of the employer's intention. It is rarely the employer's intention to discriminate: it is rather to gain a commercial advantage through the use of cheap labour. *Jenkins* was interpreted by English courts as meaning that, if the employer was motivated by commercial advantage, then that objectively justified discrimination. This would have made it difficult for part time workers to succeed under Art 141.

The effects of *Jenkins* were mitigated by *Bilka-Kaufhaus*: the ECJ held that it is for a national court to determine whether a policy is objectively justified, but it was limited by the principle of proportionality. The employer has to show that the policy:

- met a genuine need of the enterprise;
- was suitable for attaining the objective set;
- was necessary for the purpose.

Rinner-Kühn is also significant in that, although the question of objective justification is left to national courts, the ECJ is prepared to set down limits as to what can constitute justification. In particular, it will look at the merits of justification arguments. So, in *Rinner-Kühn,* the German Government could not argue that part time workers are less dependent on their earnings than full time workers.

Significant guidance as to the merits of objective justification arguments, in relation to small employers, was provided by the ECJ in a case under the Equal Treatment Directive (76/207) in *Kirsammer-Hack v Sidal* [1993], where it was held that exclusion from employment protection for part time employees of firms which had fewer than five employees was objectively justified on the ground that it lightened the administrative, financial and legal burdens on small firms.

Two German cases have also extended the rights of part time workers. In *Kowalska v Freie und Hanestadt Hamburg* [1990], it was held that a provision of a collective agreement excluding part time workers from severance pay infringed Art 119 (now Art 141). The Court also held that the national court must amend indirectly discriminatory provisions of collective agreements, as opposed to simply declaring them void.

In *Nimz v Freie und Hanestadt Hamburg* [1991], part time workers had to work twice as long for reclassification to a higher grade than full time workers. The

ECJ held that, in showing that experience is an objective factor which leads to improvement in performance, it would have to be shown that additional experience leads to better performance in the job.

The limitation of the temporal effects of *Barber* does not apply to the right to join an occupational pension scheme or to the right to payment of a retirement pension where the worker was excluded from the scheme in breach of Art 119 (now Art 141).

Consequently, part time workers have the right to join a pension scheme unless their exclusion can be objectively justified (*Vroege v NCIV* [1994]). Furthermore, this right can be backdated to 8 April 1976, which is the date of the judgment of *Defrenne (No 2)*. However, it was held in *Fisscher* [1994] that, where a pension scheme requires them, contributions can be demanded from an employee who wishes to backdate membership of the scheme for that period.

These principles were again stated in *Dietz* [1996]. The applicant, who was employed for seven hours a week, could exercise these rights directly against the administrator of the scheme, but the employee had to pay contributions for the period concerned.

SCOPE OF ART 141

Article 141 does not cover discrimination on grounds of sexual orientation. It was held in *Grant v South West Trains* [1998] that neither Art 119 (now Art 141) nor the Equal Pay Directive, Directive 75/117, covered discrimination on grounds of sexual orientation. The defendant employer had provided benefits in kind to employees in the form of travel concessions for spouses and opposite sex partners of employees but not same sex partners.

The decision, unsurprisingly, attracted a considerable amount of attention both in the media and in the legal community at the time. However, *Grant* is of largely historical interest now, following the adoption by the Council of Directive 2000/78, which prohibits, *inter alia*, sexual orientation discrimination in the employment context throughout the Community. (The Directive has been implemented into UK law by the Employment Equality (Sexual Orientation) Regulations 2003, which came into force on 1 December 2003.)

The judgment in *Grant* did not follow Advocate General Elmer's opinion and was surprising in the light of the ECJ's ruling in *P v S and Cornwall CC* [1996].

In that case, a post-operative transsexual was dismissed from her employment as a consequence of her transsexualism. The ECJ applied a purposive interpretation to Art 2(1), Directive 76/207 (the Equal Treatment Directive) and argued that the purpose of the rights it intended to protect covered gender reassignment.

Grant was not brought on the basis of Directive 76/207 and the ECJ declined to give a purposive interpretation. The judgment referred to the Treaty of Amsterdam, which gives the EC powers in the field of discrimination on grounds of sexual orientation. The ECJ felt that it was up to the Council to pass secondary legislation to give effect to these rights, which it has now done.

WHAT IS EQUAL WORK?

Article 141 is not limited to situations where the man and woman are contemporaneously employed. In *Macarthys v Smith* [1980], the applicant was paid less for the same job as her male predecessor. The ECJ also rejected the need for the adoption of a 'hypothetical male': the parallels could be drawn on the basis of 'concrete appraisals of work actually performed by employees of different sex within the establishment or service'.

'Equal work' enables applicants to compare themselves to other groups of workers who have had their work rated as inferior but still receive more pay (*Murphy v An Bord Telecom Eireann* [1987]).

EQUAL TREATMENT DIRECTIVE 2006/54 – TITLE II – EQUAL PAY

As mentioned above, Directive 2006/54 is a consolidating directive and replaces the Equal Pay Directive 75/117.

Article 4 of the new Directive prohibits discrimination and states 'For the same work or for work to which equal value is attributed, direct and indirect discrimination on grounds of sex with regard to all aspects and conditions of remuneration shall be eliminated'.

Article 14 of the new Directive provides 'there shall be no direct or indirect discrimination on grounds of sex in the public or private sectors regarding employment and working conditions, including dismissal, as well as pay as provided for in Article 141 of the Treaty'.

If a national court can identify discrimination solely by reference to Art 141, it will be directly effective. This is important because the Treaty article can be invoked both vertically and horizontally (i.e. against private employers) thus avoiding any problems which might arise regarding the direct effect of the directive.

Article 4 of the new Directive continues that where a job classification system is used for determining pay, it shall be based on the same criteria for both men and women and so drawn up as to exclude any discrimination on grounds of sex.

You will remember that under the new Directive, the respondent employer bears the burden of proof once the claimant employee has established facts from which it may be presumed that there has been direct or indirect discrimination.

Cases decided under the Equal Pay Directive 75/117 are now considered.

It was held in *Angestelltenbetriesrat der Weiner Gebietskrankenkasse v Weiner Gebietskrankenkasse* [1999] that 'same work' in Art 1, Directive 75/117 and Art 119 (now Art 141) did not apply to two groups of psychotherapists. One group held degrees in psychology, the other group were paid more and had trained as doctors. The difference in training could be an objective justification for difference in pay.

Initially, the UK implemented measures that defined equal pay as 'like work' and 'work was rated as equivalent' on the basis of a job evaluation undertaken with the consent of an employer. This was held to be a breach of the Directive in Case 61/81 *Commission v UK* [1981], as there had been a failure to provide a means whereby claims of equal value might be assessed in the absence of a job evaluation scheme. As a result, the Equal Pay (Amendment) Regulations 1983 were passed and an employment tribunal now has the power to have a report prepared to determine whether something is of equal value.

Case 143/83 *Commission v Denmark* [1983] allows for comparisons to be made with work of equal value in different establishments which are covered by the same collective agreement.

In *Rummler v Dato-Druck GmbH* [1987], a job evaluation scheme was challenged as the criteria it assessed included, *inter alia*, muscular effort. This was held not to be discriminatory so long as:

■ the system as a whole precluded discrimination;

■ the criteria used are objectively justified. In order to be classified as such they must:

● be appropriate to the tasks carried out;

● correspond to a genuine need of the undertaking.

In *Handels- og Kontorfunktionaerernes Forbund i Danmark v Dansk Arbejdsgiverforening ex p Danfoss* [1989], criteria such as 'flexibility' and 'seniority' could be taken into account in assessing pay. However, there were conditions attached to the ability to invoke 'flexibility'. If it meant that it was an assessment of the employee's work and women received less payment than men, then *prima facie* there would be discrimination and the onus would be on the employer to prove that the difference was objectively justified.

Danfoss is also interesting as it appears to accept 'seniority' as always being a reason to give more pay. This is hard to reconcile with *Nimz*, where it was held that for 'seniority' to be taken into account it would have to be shown that longer experience lead to better performance in the particular job.

SCOPE OF THE DIRECTIVE

The Equal Treatment Directive 76/207 was amended in 2002 by Directive 2002/73 but has now been repealed and replaced by the new Equal Treatment Directive 2006/54.

The original Equal Treatment Directive prohibited direct and indirect discrimination on grounds of sex and promoted equal treatment in three employment based areas:

■ access to employment and promotion;

■ vocational training;

■ working conditions

Similarly Art 14 of the new Equal Treatment Directive provides that there shall be no direct or indirect discrimination on grounds of sex in the public or private sectors, including public bodies in relation to:

- Conditions for access to employment, to self employment or to occupation including selection criteria and recruitment conditions, whatever the branch of activity and at all levels of the professional hierarchy, including promotion.

- Access to all types and to all levels of vocational guidance, vocational training, advanced vocational training and retraining, including practical work experience.

- Employment and working conditions, including dismissals as well as pay as provided for in Article 141 of the Treaty.

It can be seen that these heads mirror the former law and therefore case law decided under the Equal Treatment Directive 76/207 is now considered under the various heads.

Equality of access to employment

This was considered in *Dekker* [1991]. The applicant's offer of employment was withdrawn when the employer discovered that she was pregnant. The employer argued that the intention had not been to discriminate: there had been financial reasons behind the decision, as he would not have recovered the cost of the maternity benefit from the Dutch social fund. Nevertheless, it was held to be a breach of the Directive.

Ellis (1994) 31 CML Rev 43 argues that *Dekker* creates an extension to the idea of direct discrimination. The applicant was not recruited because she was pregnant; since only a woman can become pregnant, her sex was the cause of her failure to get the job. A causation test had been introduced to the concept of direct discrimination. Also, there was no actual male comparator in this case, so it may signal a change of mind on the question of hypothetical comparators after *Macarthys v Smith* [1980].

Despite this criticism, the correctness of *Dekker* [1991] was confirmed in *Mahlburg* [2000]. A heart clinic in Germany refused to take on M, who was pregnant, because of provisions of German law prohibiting the employment of pregnant women in certain circumstances. The clinic took the view that working in an operating theatre would expose M to the harmful effects of substances that pose a risk to health. M successfully challenged her rejection, on the basis that it contravened Directive 76/207. The Court held that 'refusal to employ a woman on account of her pregnancy cannot be justified on grounds relating to the financial loss which an employer . . . would suffer for the duration of her maternity leave. The same conclusion must be drawn as regards the financial loss caused by the fact that the woman appointed cannot be employed in the post concerned for the duration of her pregnancy'.

The case of *Adoulaye v Renault SA* [1999] involved the payment of a lump sum to female workers on commencement of maternity leave. The lump sum was argued to be discriminatory against men, as the birth of a child could have an equal financial impact upon a male employee. The court held that the payment was not discriminatory as it was designed to offset genuine occupational disadvantages inherent in maternity leave. These disadvantages included missed opportunities for promotion and a lack of knowledge of new technology. The payment was therefore accepted as a substantive measure, designed to leave women in the same position as men who were not absent from work.

The borderline between equality of access and conditions of work under the Equal Treatment Directive 76/207 (now replaced by the 2006/54 Directive) and social security under the Social Security Directive 79/7 arose in (*Jackson v Chief Adjudication Officer* [1992] and *Meyers v Adjudication Officer* [1995]).

In *Jackson*, an income support scheme, the purpose of which was to supplement the income of those with inadequate means of subsistence, could not be brought within the scope of the Equal Treatment directive solely because the method for calculating eligibility could affect a single mother's ability to take up vocational training or employment.

In *Meyers*, a condition for the award of family credit was that the claimant should be engaged in remunerative work. The aim of the benefit was to ensure that families did not find themselves worse off in work than they would have been if not working. It encouraged unemployed people to accept low paid work. Consequently, it was held to be concerned with access to employment.

Equality of access to vocational training

In *Danfoss* [1989], it was held that there was no discrimination where vocational training had been offered to a group of workers who were predominantly male, where there was an objective reason for offering it to them. In this case, it was shown that the vocational training was necessary for the tasks which had been allotted to the predominantly male employees.

Equality of working conditions (including dismissal)

Article 5, Directive 76/207 provided for the application of the equal treatment principle to working conditions and specifically stated that working conditions include dismissal.

This is repeated in Art 14 of the new Directive. The cases below were considered under Directive 76/207.

Access to a voluntary redundancy scheme came within the meaning of dismissal for the purposes of Art 5: *Burton v British Railways Board* [1982]. The applicant did not succeed in his claim as, under Art 7(1) of the Social Security Directive, it is possible to exclude from the equal treatment principle the pensionable ages for men and women. Women could apply to the voluntary redundancy scheme at the age of 50, whereas men had to wait until 55. As the ages were linked to the statutory retirement ages for men and women, it was held to be legal.

It was held in *P v S and Cornwall CC* [1996] that that Article prohibited the dismissal of a transsexual for a reason related to gender reassignment. The applicant was dismissed whilst undergoing gender reassignment and claimed to have been the victim of sex discrimination. The ECJ applied a purposive interpretation to the Directive. Art 2(1) prohibits discrimination on 'grounds of sex'. The ECJ went onto say that this is simply an expression in the relevant field of the principle of equality and that discrimination on grounds of sex was one of the fundamental human rights which the ECJ had a duty to ensure. Accordingly, the scope of the Directive could not be confined simply to discrimination based on the fact that a person was of one or other sex. In view of the purpose and the nature of the rights it sought to safeguard, it also applied to discrimination arising from gender reassignment. Where a person was dismissed on the ground of gender reassignment, he or she was to be treated unfavourably by comparison with persons of the sex to which he or she was deemed to belong before undergoing gender reassignment.

Article 7, Directive 76/207 did not apply where retirement age is calculated for 'other purposes', that is, for purposes other than eligibility for State pension:

Marshall v Southampton and South West Hampshire AHA (No 1) [1984]; *Beets-Proper v Landschot Bankiers* [1986]. In both cases, the applicants had been forced to retire at 60, whereas men could carry on until they were 65. The ages were linked to statutory retirement ages. The ECJ held that neither case concerned access to a pension scheme and the Court was therefore prepared to draw a distinction between age limits for dismissal (which comes within Art 5) and age limits for pensions (which is caught by the exemption for pensionable ages).

Conditions governing dismissal

The concept that dismissal on grounds of pregnancy is direct discrimination was confirmed in *Brown v Rentokil* [1998]. The defendants had inserted a term into the employment contract that provided that any employee who was absent from work for more than 26 weeks would be dismissed. The applicant became pregnant, was unable to work due to a pregnancy related illness and was dismissed after 26 weeks. The contractual term applied to men and women. It was held that dismissal of a woman during pregnancy on grounds of pregnancy related illness amounted to direct sex discrimination.

By contrast, in *Handels- og Kontorfunktionaerernes Forbund i Danmark (for Hertz) v Dansk Arbejdsgiverforening ex p Aldi Marked K/S* [1990], it was held that the applicant had not been unfairly dismissed for absences from work due to illness caused by a pregnancy two years earlier. The Court said that, after maternity leave, illness due to pregnancy should be treated like any other illness. The question, then, was whether she had suffered adverse treatment compared to a male employee.

Dismissal on grounds of pregnancy was again found to be discriminatory in *Webb v EMO Air Cargo (UK) Ltd* [1994]. The applicant had been employed to replace another employee who was absent on maternity leave. She was found to have been employed for an indefinite period. During the absence of her colleague on maternity leave, the applicant herself became pregnant and was unable to provide cover for the period for which she had been employed. She was then dismissed. It was held that dismissal on grounds of pregnancy of a woman employed for an indefinite period was direct discrimination. Consequently, it was not possible to justify the dismissal on the grounds that she was unable, on a temporary basis, to perform a fundamental condition of her employment contract. The protection could not be made dependent on the question of whether her presence at work during maternity was essential to the proper functioning of the undertaking in which she was employed. A contrary interpretation would render the directive ineffective. It was unclear what the position would have been if the applicant had been employed on a fixed term, as opposed to an indefinite, contract. However, Art 10 of the Pregnancy Directive 92/85 appears to give such workers protection from dismissal during the period of maternity leave.

In *Tele Danmark* [2001], the ECJ ruled that the dismissal of any pregnant woman (when the reason for the dismissal is her pregnancy) constitutes direct discrimination – regardless of whether or not she was employed on a fixed term contract. The complainant was recruited by the defendant company for a period of six months in July 1995. In August, she informed the defendant that she was pregnant and expected to give birth in early November. She was dismissed shortly afterwards. The defendant sought to argue that women on fixed term contracts were not protected by Directive 76/207, but the ECJ disagreed.

The treatment of pregnancy under equality legislation has been the subject of much criticism. Equality legislation is based on a comparison between the treatment received by a member of one sex compared to a member of the opposite sex. This framework is unsuitable for pregnancy where the needs of the sexes are different. The Pregnancy Directive 92/85 has been welcomed as it breaks away from this comparative analysis and treats pregnancy as a specific issue with special requirements. It introduces minimum protection for three categories of female workers: pregnant workers; workers who have recently given birth; and workers who are breast-feeding. It has not been amended by the new Equal Treatment Directive 2006/54.

Its provisions include protection from hazardous substances and protection from dismissal during the period of maternity leave other than in exceptional cases unconnected with pregnancy. It provides for paid time off for ante-natal examinations, minimum requirements for maternity pay, and the protection of part time and fixed term workers during the period of maternity leave.

Adoption leave is not a working condition

In Case 163/82 *Commission v Italy* [1982], the Commission took enforcement proceedings in respect of an Italian law which provided for eligibility for women but not men for three months compulsory leave after a child under the age of six was adopted into the family. This was held to be legal by the ECJ, as it was felt that it was necessary to assimilate conditions of entry of an adopted child into the family to those of a newborn child. The judgment did not follow Advocate General Rozes' opinion. She argued that the paramount aim of adoption leave is to secure the emotional ties between the child and the adoptive family. This is a task which can be performed equally as well by the father as by the mother and, therefore, in the Advocate General's opinion, it is a working condition.

DEROGATIONS FROM THE EQUAL TREATMENT PRINCIPLE

Under the former Equal Treatment Directive 76/207, there were three derogations from the equal treatment principle:

■ An occupational qualification provision.

■ A pregnancy and maternity provision.

■ Positive discrimination where it was shown that inequalities actually existed.

Occupational qualification provision

Article 14(2) of the new Equal Treatment Directive 2006/54 maintains the key features of the occupational qualification provision formerly found in Art 2(2) of Directive 76/207.

It provides that Member States may exempt occupational activities for which the sex of the worker constitutes 'a genuine and determining occupational requirement, provided that its objective is legitimate and the requirement is proportionate'.

Certain jobs require physical characteristics which determine that the job can only be done by one sex or the other, for example, actor/actress, model, wet nurse, etc.

Under Art 31(3) of the new Directive, Member States shall assess the occupational activities referred to in Art 14(2) in order to decide, in the light of social developments, whether there is justification for maintaining the exclusions concerned. They are required to notify the Commission of the results of this assessment periodically, but at least every 8 years.

There was a comparable requirement in Art 9(2) of Directive 76/207.

The significance of permitting social considerations to be taken into account is that they vary from State to State. Consequently, there is an element of discretion in the hands of a Member State as to what activities constitute excluded activities for the purpose of Art 31(3) ie the former Art 9(2).

The scope of this occupational qualification provision was considered in a number of cases under Directive 76/207.

Environment played a crucial part in the outcome of *Johnston v Chief Constable of the Royal Ulster Constabulary* [1986]. The applicant had been refused a renewal of her contract as a member of the RUC full time reserve and was not allowed to attend training in the handling and use of firearms. The reasons given for the refusal were that it was necessary for safeguarding public security and to protect public safety and public order.

The ECJ held that regard must be had to the context in which an armed police force carries out its activities, which is determined by the environment. Arming women police officers in Northern Ireland places them under a greater risk of assassination than if they are left unarmed. It was therefore contrary to the interests of public safety to provide women officers with arms. On this basis, sex was a determining factor in the carrying out of certain police activities.

The ECJ said that, even where a situation came within a derogation, there was an obligation first, under Art 9(2), to periodically assess whether the derogation could still be maintained. Secondly, as this was a derogation from an individual right, the principle of proportionality must be observed. There would have to be a balancing of the interests of equal treatment and public safety and it was for the national court to determine whether an action was proportionate or not.

In *Sirdar v Army Board* [1999], Mrs Sirdar, who had worked as an army chef since 1983, was offered a transfer to the Royal Marines after being made redundant. The offer was withdrawn when it was discovered that Mrs Sirdar was a woman. Army policy prevents women from joining the Royal Marines as every marine is expected to be capable of fighting in a commando unit at short notice. This policy exists because of the small size of Royal Marines units. It was held that the policy of excluding women in this context could be justified proportionally under Art 2(2) of the Equal Treatment Directive.

Ellis (2000) 37 CML Rev 1403 is highly critical of the *Sirdar* judgment. She says, 'the degree of gender-stereotyping . . . is little short of staggering'. *Sirdar* was distinguished soon afterwards in a superficially similar case. In *Kreil v Germany* [2000], Ms K, an electronics expert, applied for a place in the German army to work on the maintenance of electronic weapons systems. However, her application was rejected – the German Constitution prohibited women from being employed in any capacity involving the possible use of arms. (Women were only allowed to serve as medics or musicians.) The ECJ held that this prohibition was too general and could not be justified under Art 2(2).

More recently, in *Dory* [2003], both *Sirdar* and *Kreil* were distinguished. The case concerned the requirement in German law that men (but not women) must undergo compulsory military service. The Court held that, while *access to* the military was covered by the Directive, *compulsory* military service was not. This was a matter for the Member States in organising their own internal and external security.

In Case 165/82 *Commission v UK* [1982], the Commission challenged the UK's exclusion under s 6(3) of the Sex Discrimination Act 1975 from the equal treatment principle of employment in a private household or small undertakings where the number of persons does not exceed five. The Commission also challenged the UK's prohibition on men applying for employment or training as midwives. The UK Government argued that the exclusions came within Art 2(2).

The ECJ objected to the general nature of the domestic service and small business exceptions. Although there are particular jobs in both sectors which can only be performed by one particular sex, this does not justify exempting them entirely from the equal treatment principle. This was echoed in *Johnston*, where it was again held that a woman could only be excluded from specific activities.

The exclusion relating to midwives was found to be legal. The ECJ referred to Art 9(2), Directive 76/207 and the need to constantly review excluded occupational activities in the light of social developments. It was held that the exclusion was appropriate, given personal sensitivities which existed at the date of judgment. These personal sensitivities were capable of making sex a determining factor for the occupational activity. The judgment was contrary to Advocate General Rozes' opinion, who thought that there was nothing in being a midwife itself which justified the exclusion, and laid emphasis on the patient's right to choose the midwife she prefers. The UK has since allowed men to become midwives.

Protection of women, in particular with regard to pregnancy and maternity

Art 2(3) of the former Equal Treatment Directive 76/207 provided for the second exception to the equal treatment principle whereby provisions were allowed for the protection of women, particularly with regard to pregnancy and maternity.

This exception has been removed and instead Art 15 of the new Equal Treatment Directive provides that a woman on maternity leave shall be entitled, after the end of her period of maternity leave, to return to her job or to an equivalent post on terms and conditions which are no less favourable to her and to benefit from any improvement in working conditions to which she would have been entitled during her absence.

Art 16 contains a similar provision for men returning from paternity leave or for men and women returning from adoption leave.

The Pregnancy Directive 92/85 is not amended by the new Directive 2006/54.

Positive discrimination

Art 2(4) of the earlier Equal Treatment Directive 76/207 provided for positive action for women and permitted measures designed to redress inequality between men and women to promote equal opportunity for men and women and to remove existing inequalities which affected women's opportunities.

It is now dealt with by Art 3 of the new Directive 2006/54 which provides that Member States may maintain or adopt measures within the meaning of Art 141(4) of the Treaty with a view to ensuring full equality in practice between men and women in working life.

Art 141(4) of the Treaty provides that with a view to ensuring full equality in practice between men and women in working life, the principle of equal treatment shall not prevent any Member State from maintaining or adopting measures providing for specific advantages in order to make it easier for the underrepresented sex to pursue a vocational activity or to prevent or compensate for disadvantages in professional careers.

149

It is believed that although the wording is slightly different from the wording in the Equal Treatment Directive 76/207, the ECJ will interpret it in a similar fashion, ie strictly.

The ECJ would only permit positive discrimination where it could be shown that inequalities actually existed.

In *Kalanke v Freie Hanestadt Bremen* [1996], the ECJ ruled that national rules which guarantee women absolute and unconditional priority for appointment or promotion, go beyond equal opportunities and exceed the positive action permitted under Art 2(4). The Commission has asserted that it makes only rigid quota systems illegal.

A different result was achieved in *Marschall v Land Nordrhein Westfalen* [1997]. The case concerned a German regional law which provided that, where there were fewer women than men in a higher grade post, women were to be given priority in the event of equal suitability, competence and professional performance unless there were reasons specific to an individual male candidate that tilted matters in his favour. The 'saving clause' led to the ECJ holding that the law came within Art 2(4), Directive 76/207 as it allowed for an assessment of individual circumstances.

Both of these rulings were confirmed subsequently. *Kalanke* was followed in *Abrahamsson and Anderson v Fogelqvist* [2000], involving Swedish law conferring priority on female applicants for professorial posts at Swedish universities. This was held to be contrary to the Directive, because there was no saving clause.

Marschall was applied in both *Badeck* [2000] and *Lommers* [2002]. The latter case involved Dutch rules conferring priority on creche places for infants to female employees. Mr L challenged this but the ECJ held that it was justifiable. The provision had a similar saving clause to that in *Marschall*, in that fathers could be awarded a creche place for their children in an 'emergency'.

Finally on this point, in *Schnorbus* [2000], the ECJ held that Art 2(4) also applies to measures designed to positively discriminate in favour of men. Ms S had applied for a training post with the Ministry of Justice in Hesse, Germany, but had her application deferred because they were oversubscribed. German law conferred priority in such situations on those for whom deferral would constitute 'particular hardship'. One example of hardship was men who may be disadvantaged because of the requirement in German law that men (but not women) must undergo compulsory military service. The Court held that the German rules were acceptable.

The concept of positive discrimination in Community law has been extended by its inclusion in the agreement annexed to the Social Protocol of the Treaty on European Union. Article 6(3) allows for measures of positive discrimination.

EFFECTIVE REMEDIES

Starting with the cases of *Von Colson and Kamman v Land Nordrhein Westfalen* [1984] and *Harz v Deutsche Tradaz* [1984], it can be seen that the directive requires real and effective sanctions where there has been a breach of the equal treatment principle. Although there is no express provision to this effect in the directive, Art 6, Directive 76/207 requires the Member States to introduce measures so that applicants who feel wronged by the failure to apply the equal treatment to them can pursue their claims by judicial process. From this, the ECJ has adduced the need for effective sanctions, and said in its judgment in *Von Colson* that 'it is impossible to establish real equality of opportunity without an appropriate system of sanctions'.

The principle was applied in relation to British legislation in *Marshall v Southampton and South West Hampshire AHA (No 2)* [1993]. An arbitrary upper limit of £6,250 compensation in the Sex Discrimination Act 1975 for the victim of discrimination was held to be contrary to Art 6 of the Equal Treatment Directive. The ECJ held that, where financial compensation is the method of fulfilling the Directive's objectives, it must enable the financial loss and damage actually suffered to be made good. In this respect, the judgment differed from Advocate General Gerven's opinion, which had stated that although the damages must be 'adequate' they did not have to be equal to the damage suffered. The court also said that an award of damages could not leave out matters such as 'effluxion of time' which might reduce the value of the award, and therefore interest was payable on the damages. Finally, it was also held that for limited purposes Art 6 had direct effect. Where a Member State has been free to choose from amongst a number of solutions which are suitable for achieving the objective of the directive and has made its choice, then Art 6 may be relied on.

Procedural remedies

In addition to substantive remedies such as damages, a case under the Social Security Directive, *Emmott v Minister of Social Welfare* [1991], held that it is also necessary to create effective procedural remedies. In that case it was held that limitation periods do not start to run until a directive is properly implemented.

EQUAL TREATMENT DIRECTIVE 2006/54 – TITLE III

In Title III of the new Directive, there are now provisions relating to equality bodies, remedies, compliance, etc. which bring this sex equality secondary legislation into line with other anti-discriminatory directives, eg covering race, disability, etc.

You should now be confident that you would be able to tick all of the boxes on the checklist at the beginning of this chapter. To check your knowledge of EC sex equality legislation why not visit the companion website and take the Multiple Choice Question test. Check your understanding of the terms and vocabulary used in this chapter with the flashcard glossary.

7

Free movement of goods

Appreciate the different ways in which the free movement of goods can be hindered ☐

Distinguish between customs duties and charges having equivalent effect and explain how they are regulated by the EC Treaty ☐

Distinguish between quantitative restrictions and measures having equivalent effect ☐

Discuss the rule of reason introduced in *Cassis de Dijon* ☐

Explain the decision in *Keck* and *Mithouard* ☐

Explain when a Member State may rely on the Art 30 derogations ☐

INTRODUCTION

The free movement of goods is possibly the central aspect of the EU's internal market. The principle of free movement of goods is achieved by three separate means:

1 prohibition of customs duties between Member States – Art 23;
2 prohibition of quantitative restrictions on imports and exports between Member States – Arts 28 and 29;
3 prohibition of discriminatory taxation between Member States – Art 90.

Before looking at these in depth, it is helpful to understand what 'goods' means under EC law. 'Goods' are defined very widely. According to the ECJ in *Commission v Italy* [1968]:

> By 'goods' ... there must be understood products which can be valued in money, and which are capable, as such, of forming the subject of commercial transactions.

Thus anything which can be bought or sold is 'goods'. In *Commission v Belgium* [1992], the ECJ rejected an argument put forward by Belgium that waste could not be 'goods'. Anything shipped across a border for the purposes of commercial transactions was covered.

The free movement provisions apply equally to goods manufactured or produced in the EU and to those in free circulation there, regardless of their country of origin (*Donckerwolcke* [1976]).

CUSTOMS UNION

According to Art 23, 'the Community shall be based upon a customs union which shall cover all trade in goods and which shall involve the prohibition between Member States of customs duties on imports and exports and of all charges having equivalent effect, and the adoption of a common customs tariff in their relations with third countries'. Art 23 is directly effective (*Van Gend en Loos* [1963]).

Article 23 therefore creates the Customs Union. It has two parts:

1 common customs tariff;
2 prohibition on customs duties between Member States.

COMMON CUSTOMS TARIFF (CCT)

The CCT applies to all goods imported into the EU from countries such as Japan and the USA. The Commission sets the level of the tariff for each product. This led to a threatened trade war with the United States in the early months of 1999, as the Commission had set a lower tariff for bananas imported from former British colonies in the West Indies than for bananas imported from Central and South American countries, where many US-controlled banana plantations are based. The tariffs collected by each State's customs authorities are paid into the EU's central budget.

PROHIBITION OF CUSTOMS DUTIES BETWEEN MEMBER STATES

Article 23 states that the Customs Union involves a prohibition on 'Customs duties on imports or exports' and 'charges having equivalent effect' between Member States. This prevents Member States from charging importers for bringing goods into that State from another Member State, whether the goods were produced in the EU or not.

Art 25 (described as the 'standstill' provision) prohibits the introduction between Member States of any new customs duties on imports or exports or any charges having equivalent effect.

What are 'customs duties' and 'charges having equivalent effect'?

A customs duty is any charge that is imposed on goods because they are imported (*Steinike & Weinleg* [1977]). Article 23 prohibits these charges because they may have the effect of reducing imports, and hence trade, by making imported goods more expensive. A simple prohibition on customs duties would have allowed customs authorities to continue to charge importers through less obvious means. Hence Art 23 also prohibits charges having 'equivalent effect' to customs duties. Any pecuniary charge, whatever its size and name, imposed on any goods by reason of the fact that they cross a frontier, and which is not a customs duty in the strict sense, is a 'charge having equivalent effect' (*Commission v Italy* [1969]).

Many customs duties are imposed to make imports relatively more expensive and hence protect domestic production. But there is no requirement that the charge be levied for protectionist reasons. There may even be no domestic market in need of protection; but this will not stop the charge from infringing

Art 23. In *Sociaal Fonds voor de Diamantarbeiders* [1969], a charge of 1/3 per cent was imposed on unworked diamonds imported into Belgium. The purpose was to raise funds for workers in the diamond-mining industry in Africa. Various importers of industrial diamonds challenged the charge. Following a reference from the Belgian court, the ECJ held that the charge contravened Art 23.

When a breach of Art 23 is established after duties or equivalent changes have been paid, then the Member State in question is, in principle, obliged to repay the importer/exporter, as the case may be (*San Giorgio* [1983]; *Dilexport* [1999]). Moreover, national rules of evidence which have the effect of making it virtually impossible or excessively difficult to secure repayment of duties or equivalent charges levied in breach of Art 23 are incompatible with EU law (*San Giorgio*). However, EU law does not require the repayment of the duty or equivalent charge in circumstances where this would unjustly enrich the person concerned (*Just* [1980]). This would occur in a situation, for example, where the burden of the charge has been transferred in whole or in part to other persons. Thus, if an importer had paid the duty or equivalent charge, but then passed on the cost to the distributor of the goods in the importing State, then to order repayment to the importer would over-compensate them (*Société Comatelo & Others* [1997]).

What if the charges are for services carried out for the benefit of the importer?
A charge for services which benefit the community in general, eg health inspections or quality control, is nevertheless in breach of Art 23 (*Rewe-Zentralfinanz* [1973]).

A charge which is imposed for services provided to the importer/exporter by the customs authorities (for example, warehouse facilities) may be compatible with Art 23, provided that the services give a 'tangible benefit' to the importer/exporter, and the charge does not exceed the cost of the service. In *Donner* [1983], the Dutch Post Office charged Andreas Donner a fee for dealing with the payment of VAT on a number of books he had imported into the Netherlands. This was held by the ECJ to be capable of being regarded as payment for services and therefore permissible.

What if charges are for services imposed under EC law?
Where the services charged for are imposed under EU law, then a charge could

be regarded as a payment for services and therefore it would be permissible for the State to require payment of it (*Bauhuis* [1977]). Where the State is permitted to charge for services, it is only entitled to recover the actual cost of the service, and no more (*Denkavit* [1982]).

PROHIBITION OF QUANTITATIVE RESTRICTIONS ON IMPORTS AND MEASURES HAVING EQUIVALENT EFFECT: ART 28

A simple abolition of customs duties under Art 23 would not have been sufficient to guarantee the free movement of goods. There are an infinite variety of legal, administrative and procedural practices that may be adopted by Member States that have the *effect* of reducing intra-Community trade. Art 28 is designed to eliminate these practices.

Article 28 provides that 'Quantitative restrictions on imports and all measures having equivalent effect shall . . . be prohibited between Member States'. (Art 29 provides the same for exports.) A national law or measure that infringes Art 28 is *prima facie* contrary to EU law; however Art 30 provides that Art 28 will not apply to certain restrictions which are justifiable on various grounds. In addition to these derogations, the ECJ has developed its own line of case law, in which it has held that certain measures will not breach Art 28 if they are necessary to satisfy mandatory requirements, ie national rules which may be raised by Member States as justification for overriding Art 28. This is known as the 'rule of reason', and was introduced in *Cassis de Dijon* [1979]. Further as will be seen below in *Keck and Mithouard* [1993], the ECJ has confirmed that national laws which relate to 'Selling Arrangements' are outside of the scope of Art 28 altogether. All of these aspects of EU law on the free movement of goods will be considered in detail below.

Although Art 28 is directly effective, it is important to note that it is addressed to, and only relates to measures taken by, or on behalf of, the Member States. 'State' has, however, been given a very wide meaning. It includes, for example:

■ national and local government, in its many forms;

■ semi-public bodies such as quangos (eg *Apple & Pear Development Council v KJ Lewis Ltd* [1983]);

■ the post office (*Commission v France* [1985]);

■ the police force (*R v Chief Constable of Sussex ex p International Traders' Ferry Ltd* [1998], House of Lords).

In *R v Pharmaceutical Society of GB ex p Association of Pharmaceutical Importers* [1989] the ECJ held that rules established by regulatory agencies and professional bodies established under statutory authority may also be subject to the control of EU law.

'Quantitative restrictions'

A 'quantitative restriction' has been defined as any measure which amounts to a total, or partial, restraint on imports, exports or goods in transit (*Riseria Luigi Geddo v Ente Nazionale Risi* [1973]). This most obviously includes a quota system (*Salgoil* [1968]), but also includes an outright ban on imports (*Commission v Italy* [1961]; *R v Henn and Darby* [1979]).

'Measures having equivalent effect' to quantitative restrictions (MEQR)

The classic formulation of what is meant by MEQR was given by the ECJ in *Dassonville* [1974]:

All trading rules enacted by Member States which are capable of hindering, directly or indirectly, actually or potentially, intra-Community trade are to be considered as measures having an effect equivalent to quantitative restrictions.

This has become known as the *Dassonville* 'formula'. The definition given to 'measures having an effect equivalent to quantitative restrictions' is very wide and means that virtually any measure which limits imports or exports in any way could be caught by Art 28 and Art 29.

Examples of MEQRs

The following is a list of examples of national laws that have been held to be prohibited by Art 28. This is *not* a comprehensive list. Remember that many of these laws are capable of justification under either Art 30 or the *Cassis de Dijon* principle.

■ A classic method adopted by Member States to introduce import restrictions is to insist on importers being licensed. These are often held to be justified on health grounds. Nevertheless, the ECJ has consistently held that such requirements are *prima facie* in breach of Art 28. The reasons are twofold: first, because applying for licences is a time-consuming process, importers will be unable to import goods while awaiting their licence; secondly, some importers may be disinclined to go to the trouble of applying for a licence. If even one potential importer decides not to apply for a licence, then there has been a restriction on imports. One such case, *Commission v UK* [1983], will be considered below.

■ National rules requiring goods to be marked with their country of origin could also infringe Art 28 because that would impose extra burdens on importers, many of whom would not necessarily be aware of the national law and so face difficulties in complying with it. In *Dassonville* itself, D was a trader in Belgium who imported a consignment of Johnnie Walker and Vat 69 Scotch whisky from France. Under Belgian law, a certificate of origin was required for all imports of a range of goods, including Scotch whisky. France had no such legislation and the French distributor was unable to provide a certificate of origin, which could only be issued by the UK customs authorities. Despite this, D went ahead with the transaction, using forged documents. The Belgian authorities discovered the forgery and D was prosecuted. He pleaded Art 28 in his defence, and the Belgian court referred the matter to the ECJ, which found that the Belgian law infringed Art 28.

▶ PROCUREUR DU ROI v DASSONVILLE (Case 8/74)

Under Belgian law, a certificate of origin was required for Scotch whisky. This could only be issued by UK customs. *Dassonville* **imported Scotch whisky into Belgium through France and forged a certificate of origin. When he was prosecuted he pleaded that the requirement for such a certificate constituted a MEQR and was therefore prohibited under Art 28 EC Treaty.**

The ECJ held that the requirement did constitute a MEQR which it described as 'all trading rules enacted by Member States which are capable of hindering, directly or indirectly, actually or potentially, intra-Community trade'.

■ Government-sponsored campaigns to encourage consumers to buy domestic products clearly infringe Art 28. This is because they have the potential (at least) to influence traders and shoppers into discriminating against imports and thus frustrating free movement. In *Commission v Ireland* [1982], the Irish Goods Council was a semi-public body given the task by the Irish Government of promoting Irish goods on the basis of their Irish origin. The Council was given financial support to launch a major advertising campaign by the Irish Ministry of Industry. The activities of the Council were held to have infringed Art 28.

■ However, *Commission v Ireland* was distinguished in *Apple & Pear Development Council v KJ Lewis Ltd* [1983]. The Council had been set up to promote the consumption of apples and pears grown in England and Wales *via* a television advertising campaign (using the slogan 'Polish up your English') and research projects. Several growers refused to pay the levy due, and were sued by the Council. In their defence they argued Art 28. The ECJ held that it was permissible to promote a national product by reference to its particular qualities, but not simply because it was from a particular State. The EU's internal market rules encourage competition based on quality, but not nationality.

■ National laws which relate to how products are packaged may well infringe Art 28, because they increase the costs of manufacturers in other Member States, who may have to develop special packaging processes purely for the importing State. It may also inhibit distributors and retailers in that State from importing goods that do not comply with the national law. Conversely, it will be much easier for domestic manufacturers to comply with their own national requirements as to packaging. In *Walter Rau v De Smedt* [1982], Belgian law prohibited the sale of margarine otherwise than in cubes, ostensibly to help consumers distinguish such products from butter. Rau, a German company, contracted to supply De Smedt, a Belgian supermarket chain, with 15,000 kg of margarine. When the margarine was delivered it was in truncated cone-shaped containers. De Smedt, aware of the requirements of Belgian law, refused to accept delivery. Rau sued for specific performance of the contract. On a reference to the ECJ, the Court ruled that the Belgian law was a measure equivalent to a quantitative restriction and therefore infringed Art 28.

Selling arrangements

One problem with the *Dassonville* 'formula' is its failure to distinguish between national laws that regulate goods themselves, and national laws that regulate how goods are sold. Various academic commentators had pointed out that this distinction should be drawn, but it was not until 1993 that the ECJ finally made this distinction. The result of that judgment – *Keck and Mithouard* [1993] – is that it is necessary to draw a distinction between two categories of national law:

1   laws regulating the goods themselves, such as weights and measures, packaging, ingredients, etc. Such laws may be referred to as 'product requirements' and are MEQRs. They are, therefore, prohibited by Art 28 (*Dassonville* applies), unless justified, either under Art 30 or *Cassis* principles (see below); and

2   laws concerning not the goods themselves, but rather when and/or where they are sold. Such laws may be referred to as 'selling arrangements' and are not MEQRs. They are, therefore, not prohibited by Art 28 (*Keck and Mithouard* applies) and so do not require justification, under either Art 30 or *Cassis* principles.

The reason for the distinction is a simple one. Product requirements impose obstacles to trade, and therefore undermine the principle of the free movement of goods. Hence Art 28 applies. Selling arrangements, on the other hand, do not impose obstacles to trade.

> ### ▶ REWE ZENTRALE AG (the Cassis case) (Case 120/78)
>
> **German legislation laid down a minimum alcohol level of 25 per cent for cassis. Rewe-Zentrale, a German company, which sought to import French cassis with an alcohol level of approximately 20 per cent argued that the German legislation contravened Art 28. Germany pleaded grounds of consumer protection.**
>
> **The ECJ established the rule of reason to the effect that a measure may not come within Art 28 if it could be justified. However, it went on to rule that the German legislation was not necessary to achieve the aim of consumer protection.**

In *Keck and Mithouard* [1993] K and M, two supermarket managers in France, were prosecuted under French law for re-selling products (coffee and beer, respectively) lower than their purchase price. Such laws are designed to stop powerful companies from abusing their position and distorting the market by undercutting smaller rivals. K and M argued that the French law hindered EU trade. The ECJ began by citing *Dassonville*, and acknowledged that the French law 'may restrict the volume of sales ... insofar as it deprives traders of a method of sales promotion'. However, in view of the increasing tendency of traders to seek to avoid non-protectionist national laws by relying on Art 28, the ECJ decided to review its position. It concluded that (para 16):

> ... contrary to what has previously been decided, the application to products ... of national provisions restricting or prohibiting certain selling arrangements is not such as to hinder, directly or indirectly, actually or potentially, trade between Member States with the meaning of the *Dassonville* judgment, so long as those provisions apply to all relevant traders operating within the national territory and so long as they affect in the same manner, in law and in fact, the marketing of domestic products and of those from other Member States. Where these conditions are fulfilled, the application of such rules to the sale of products from another Member State meeting the requirements laid down by that State is not by nature such as to prevent their access to the market or to impede access any more than it impedes the access of domestic products. Such rules therefore fall outside the scope of Art 30.

Thus, national laws which only regulate 'selling arrangements' – how, when, or where goods are sold – in an entirely neutral manner are outside the scope of Art 28 altogether. This new approach has been confirmed in a variety of cases since 1993. It is also possible to look back over the ECJ's pre-1993 case law and identify a number of cases that would be decided differently now. This is why, in *Keck and Mithouard*, the Court used the phrase 'contrary to what has previously been decided' at the start of para 16 of its judgment. It is now possible to identify a variety of national laws that will be classed as 'selling arrangements'.

> ▶ CRIMINAL PROCEEDINGS AGAINST KECK AND MITHOUARD (Cases C-267 and 268/91)
>
> **Two supermarket managers were prosecuted for re-selling coffee and beer for lower than their purchase price. This was an offence under French law but the managers claimed that the law was**

> **contrary to Art 28 which prohibits measures equivalent to quantitative restrictions.**
>
> The ECJ ruled that the French law constituted 'selling arrangements' and was outside the scope of Art 28.

In *Tankstation t'Heukske & JBE Boermans* [1994], Dutch legislation required all shops to close during the night (subject to certain limited exceptions, eg for petrol stations). Two Dutch traders were prosecuted and convicted for breaching this rule. On appeal, they argued that the Dutch rules imposed a restriction on intra-State trade. The ECJ disagreed: following *Keck and Mithouard*, the Dutch rules simply constituted a selling arrangement.

Commission v Greece [1995] involved Greek legislation imposing a requirement that powdered milk for infants was only to be sold in pharmacists' shops. In *Banchero* [1996], Italian law reserved the sale of tobacco products to authorised retail outlets only. Both national rules were held to be selling arrangements.

Prior to *Keck and Mithouard* there was a series of cases examining the compatibility of Sunday trading laws with Art 28 (ie national laws prohibiting some, or most, shops from opening on Sundays). Such laws are certainly capable of infringing Art 28, because they reduce the trading freedom of retailers and consumers. One such law was s 47 of the UK's Shops Act 1950, which prevented the sale of certain items on Sundays until the British Parliament decided to relax the rules with effect from August 1994 by the Sunday Trading Act 1994. In both *Torfaen Borough Council v B&Q plc* [1989] and *Stoke-on-Trent City Council v B&Q plc* [1992] the ECJ ruled that s 47 constituted a MEQR (although it was justifiable under *Cassis* principles). However, following *Keck and Mithouard*, in *Punto Casa & PPV* [1994] and *Semararo Casa Uno* [1996], both concerning Italian Sunday trading legislation, the Court decided that Sunday trading laws were selling arrangements.

The most controversial aspect of selling arrangements concerns advertising restrictions. In both *Hünermund* [1993] – German law banning pharmacists from advertising on the radio, on TV or at the cinema – and *Leclerc-Siplec* [1995] – French law prohibiting television advertising in the distribution sector – the ECJ ruled that Art 28 did not apply. However, since those two cases, the

6

ECJ has drawn a distinction between partial advertising bans (eg no TV advertising), which amount to selling arrangements; and complete advertising bans, which do not. The Court indicated that a complete advertising ban may amount to a breach of Art 28 in *De Agostini & TV-Shop* [1997]. In Sweden, advertising designed to attract the attention of children aged under 12 is completely banned. The ECJ considered that this might not satisfy the condition in *Keck and Mithouard* that 'provisions apply to all relevant traders operating within the national territory and so long as they affect in the same manner, in law and in fact, the marketing of domestic products and of those from other Member States', although it left resolution of this point to the Swedish courts.

In a more recent case, the Court decided that another Swedish advertising law, effectively prohibiting any advertising of alcohol, definitely did infringe Art 28. In *Gourmet International Products* [2001] the ECJ found that this was likely to have a greater impact on imported alcoholic products than on Swedish alcoholic products, with which Swedish consumers were more familiar. The Court said:

> . . . a prohibition of all advertising . . . is liable to impede access to the market by products from other Member States more than it impedes access by domestic products, with which consumers are instantly more familiar . . . A prohibition on advertising . . . must therefore be regarded as affecting the marketing of products from other Member States more heavily than the marketing of domestic products and as therefore constituting an obstacle to trade between Member States . . .

The effect of this ruling is that the Swedish law constitutes a MEQR, although one that is capable of being justified under Art 30 (see below). In the UK, similar legislation has recently come into effect prohibiting all tobacco advertising – the Tobacco Advertising and Promotion Act 2002. It is likely that this legislation would (if it were ever challenged) be dealt with in a similar way to the Swedish alcohol advertising restrictions.

PROHIBITION OF QUANTITATIVE RESTRICTIONS ON EXPORTS: ART 29

Article 29 provides that 'Quantitative restrictions on exports, and all measures having equivalent effect, shall be prohibited between Member States'. Under Art 29 the *Dassonville* formula does not apply. In order to breach Art 29, national laws must be protectionist, that is, national laws must have the restriction of exports as their specific object or effect. This was established in *Groenveld* [1979]. Dutch law banned the possession of horsemeat by the manufacturers of meat products. When one such manufacturer brought a challenge to the Dutch rules alleging a breach of Art 29, the ECJ held there had been no breach, because the law drew no distinction between meat products destined for the Dutch market and those intended for export.

Conversely, in *Bouhelier* [1977], French law imposed a licensing system on certain watches – but only those intended for export. The ECJ held that this did constitute a breach of Art 29. Similarly, in *R v Thompson* [1978], where UK law banned the exportation of silver coins, and in *Dusseldorp* [1998], where Dutch law restricted the exportation of certain waste products for recycling, both were held to constitute a breach of Art 29.

DEROGATION FROM ARTS 28 AND 29: ART 30

The drafters of the EC Treaty recognised that many national laws might have the effect of preventing imports but that there might be overriding reasons why the national law should prevail over Community law. Hence, Art 30 provides that certain national laws may be justified on various grounds.

Art 30 provides:

> The provisions of Arts 28 and 29 shall not preclude prohibitions or restrictions on imports, exports or goods in transit justified on grounds of public morality, public policy or public security; the protection of health and life of humans, animals or plants; the protection of national treasures possessing artistic, historic or archaeological value; or the protection of industrial or commercial property. Such prohibitions or restrictions shall not, however, constitute a means of arbitrary discrimination or a disguised restriction on trade between Member States.

The grounds listed are exhaustive and may not be added to (*Commission v Italy* [1982]). Moreover, the grounds have been restrictively interpreted, because they operate as exceptions to the fundamental principle, that of the free movement of goods.

The grounds under Art 30

Public morality

Public morality is something for Member States to decide in accordance with their own values. This principle was established in *R v Henn and Darby* [1979]. The defendants had imported a consignment of pornographic films and magazines into the UK from Denmark. Most of the films and magazines were lawfully produced and marketed in Denmark. However, the consignment was detected by British customs at Felixstowe and the defendants were arrested. They were jointly convicted of being 'knowingly concerned in the fraudulent evasion of the prohibition of the importation of obscene articles', under the UK's Customs Consolidation Act 1876. On appeal, they argued that Art 28 provided a defence, while the prosecution invoked Art 30 to justify the UK customs legislation. The Court of Appeal rejected their appeal but, on further appeal to the House of Lords, a reference was made to the ECJ. The Court held that the 1876 Act was subject to Art 28 but was justifiable under Art 30. The measure was genuinely applied for the protection of British public morality.

Public policy

Despite potential width, this has rarely been successfully invoked. However, in *R v Thompson* [1978], a restriction on the exportation of silver coins from the UK was justified on public policy grounds, since the State had an interest in protecting its mint coinage.

Public security

This ground is also rarely pleaded successfully in defence of national laws. One such case was *Campus Oil* [1982]. Irish law required importers of petroleum oils to buy 35 per cent of their petrol from the Irish National Petroleum Company, at fixed prices. Although the law was discriminatory, and protective, it was held to be justified. The law was necessary to maintain a viable refinery in Ireland that could meet the nation's essential needs in the event of a crisis. Supplies of petroleum for fuel and other uses was of fundamental importance to a country's existence, since it was needed not only for the economy, but for its inhabitants, including the emergency services.

Protection of the health and life of humans, animals and plants

This ground has, unsurprisingly, been utilised to try to justify many national rules and measures. It has, however, been held that there must be a 'real health risk'. This will not be the case if the exporting State maintains equivalent standards. In *Commission v UK* [1983], UK law required that ultra heat-treated milk be marketed by approved dairies only – allegedly to ensure milk was free from bacterial infection – which necessitated the reheating and repackaging of imported milk. This law was held to be unjustified. Nor was an import licence justified. There was evidence that imported milk was of similar quality, and subject to the same standards, as UK milk.

There must also be a 'seriously considered health policy' in the State seeking to restrict imports. In *Commission v UK* [1982], the UK government announced a prohibition on the importation of poultry meat and eggs from all Member States except Ireland and Denmark. The ostensible aim of the prohibition was to prevent the spread of 'Newcastle disease' by only allowing imports from those States, ie Ireland and Denmark, with a slaughtering policy in the event of an outbreak of the disease. The ECJ found that the prohibition was unjustified, on the ground that there was no 'seriously considered health policy'. There had been little in the way of research, reports or studies. Rather, there was evidence showing that the prohibition followed domestic pressure to restrict growing imports of French poultry, especially as it was timed to coincide with Christmas and thus prevent the sale of French turkeys in the UK.

The majority of cases involve imports of food and drink, but Art 30 has wider scope than that. In *Toolex Alpha* [2000], Swedish law prohibited the sale and use of chemical products composed wholly or partially of a chemical called trichloroethylene (TE). According to the Swedish government, the chemical was carcinogenic, that is, it posed a risk of cancer in humans as well as posing a threat to the environment. Toolex Alpha, a manufacturer of machine parts used in the production of CDs, used TE to remove residues of grease produced during the manufacturing process. They challenged the Swedish rules, alleging a breach of Art 28. The Swedish government successfully relied upon Art 30.

The ECJ in *Greenham & Abel* [2004] issued important new guidelines on the scope of the health derogation, particularly designed for use in cases where products are not universally banned throughout the EU but are only banned in certain states. The case involved French legislation prohibiting the sale of adulterated food. Under the legislation, certain substances were banned (including a chemical substance called Q10). Two men had been charged with selling a product called 'Juice Plus', to which Q10 had been added. The men claimed that Q10 had been in free circulation in Spain and Italy since 1995 and in Germany and the UK since 2000. They therefore maintained that the French prohibition of Q10 breached Article 28. The ECJ responded that national rules restricting imports where justification is sought on health grounds 'must be based on a detailed assessment of the risk to public health, based on the most reliable scientific data available and the most recent results of international research'. Whether the rules were in fact justified was a question for the national courts.

Protection of national treasures
For example, a national law preventing art treasures leaving a country might be justified (see *Commission v Italy* [1968]). This ground would probably only apply to exports.

Protection of industrial and commercial property
This covers intellectual property rights: copyright, trade marks and patents, and is beyond the scope of this book.

'Arbitrary' discrimination
Even if a measure is covered by Art 30, it will still be unlawful if it amounts to 'arbitrary' discrimination. In *Conegate Ltd* [1986], a British company had imported inflatable rubber dolls into the UK from Germany. A number of consignments of dolls and other sex articles were seized at Gatwick Airport by HM customs officers under the Customs Consolidation Act 1876 (the same legislation as in *R v Henn and Darby* [1979]). The company brought an action for recovery of the dolls, relying on Art 28. The customs authorities relied on Art 30. However, the ECJ held that Art 30 did not apply because, although the sale of such products was restricted in the UK (to licensed sex shops and mail order outlets), it was not banned. Therefore, to refuse importation of the German dolls when practically identical products were on sale in the UK would constitute arbitrary discrimination.

A 'disguised restriction on trade'
A national law that would otherwise be protected by Art 30 may be castigated as a disguised restriction on trade. An example would be the import ban on French poultry in *Commission v UK* [1982], above.

Proportionality
The grounds of exemption under Article 30 appear generous. However, the ECJ

has consistently held that the purpose of the Article is to allow certain national laws and rules to derogate from the free movement provisions only to the extent to which they are 'justified' in order to achieve the objectives in the Article. A measure may be justified provided it does what is necessary to achieve the objectives in the first sentence of Art 30, and further that it does no more than necessary. If there are other methods capable of achieving that objective which are less restrictive of intra-Community trade, then they should be used instead. In *De Peijper* [1976], for example, the ECJ said:

> . . . national rules or practices which do restrict imports . . . or are capable of doing so are only compatible with the Treaty to the extent to which they are *necessary* . . . National rules or practices do not fall within the exemptions specified in [Art 30] if [their objectives] can as effectively be protected by measures which do not restrict intra-Community trade so much.

Relationship between Art 30 and harmonising directives

Where harmonising directives in a particular area have been adopted, Member States may not unilaterally adopt, on their own authority, corrective or protective measures designed to obviate any breach by another Member State of EU law. In *Hedley Lomas* [1996] – discussed in Chapter 2 – the ECJ held that recourse to Art 30 (on grounds of protection of animal health) was not possible because of the presence of Directive 74/577 regulating conditions in slaughterhouses throughout the EU.

NON-DISCRIMINATORY NATIONAL RULES AND OBJECTIVE JUSTIFICATION: THE 'RULE OF REASON'

The *Dassonville* formula (discussed above) is so wide that it catches a lot of perfectly sensible and fair national laws that have nothing to do with protectionism. It catches not just discriminatory, protectionist national laws, but non-discriminatory, non-protectionist national laws as well, without distinguishing between them. Obviously, Art 30 is available in some cases but it must be remembered that Art 30 was written in the late 1950s. By the late 1970s, many EC states had unilaterally developed sophisticated consumer protection and unfair competition laws – and those laws were more than capable of imposing restrictions on the free movement of goods. Were all of these laws automatically prohibited by Art 28?

The ECJ sought to address these problems in the landmark case of *Cassis de Dijon* [1979]. The Court began by quoting *Dassonville*, but added that:

Obstacles to movement within the Community resulting from disparities between the national laws relating to the marketing of the products in question must be accepted in so far as these provisions may be recognised as being necessary in order to satisfy mandatory requirements relating in particular to the effectiveness of fiscal supervision, the protection of public health, the fairness of commercial transactions and the defence of the consumer.

Prior to *Cassis*, national laws that were found to be in breach of Art 28, as defined in *Dassonville*, could only be justified under Art 30. After *Cassis*, national laws could be saved either by the 'rule of reason' or by Art 30. However – and this point is extremely important – in *Gilli & Andres* [1980], the ECJ stated that *Cassis* only operated to save those national laws that apply 'without discrimination' to domestic and imported products. Discriminatory national laws, eg those that apply to imports only, or which apply different rules to imports and domestic goods may only be saved by using Art 30.

In *Cassis*, Rewe-Zentrale, a firm of German importers, wanted to import a French blackcurrant liqueur (called cassis) with an alcohol content of about 15–20 per cent proof. They applied to the German authorities for permission but were informed that the French cassis was of insufficient alcoholic strength. German law laid down a minimum alcohol level of 25 per cent per litre for cassis. When Rewe challenged the German law, the case was referred to the ECJ, giving the Court the opportunity to create the 'rule of reason'.

The mandatory requirements

In *Cassis de Dijon* [1979], the ECJ referred to 'mandatory requirements' ie national rules which may be raised by Member States as justification for over-riding Art 28 if there is a very good reason for doing so. In *Cassis de Dijon*, the Court listed four grounds 'in particular', implying that its list was not closed. Indeed, the four grounds given in *Cassis* have since been added to subsequently. There is nothing to stop one of the Member States, when it finds its laws challenged, from arguing one – or sometimes more than one – mandatory requirement as a defence. Some of the grounds are argued more often than others.

Fairness of commercial transactions

In *Prantl* [1984], P was prosecuted under German unfair competition law for importing Italian wine in bottles, which were very similar in shape and design to distinctively-shaped German bottles protected under the German law as designating a particular quality wine. In his defence, P argued Art 28; the German authorities tried to claim that the law was justified in the interests of fair trading. The ECJ held that as the bottles were fairly and traditionally manufactured in Italy, there was no justification for excluding them from Germany.

Defence of the consumer

Several cases have been argued on this ground, including *Walter Rau v De Smedt* [1982] which was discussed above, and *Clinique* [1994], which will be examined below.

Protection of cultural and socio-cultural characteristics

In *Cinéthèque* [1985], French legislation prohibited the marketing of videos within 12 months of first being shown at the cinema. C, a French video distributor, had acquired the rights to distribute a video in October 1983. However, the film had only been released at the French cinema in June. C challenged the law and the case was referred to the ECJ, which accepted the restriction was justified, and the law was not in breach of Art 28. The Court referred to the 'protection of the cinema as a means of cultural expression, which protection was necessary in view of the rapid development of other modes of film distribution'.

Protection of the environment

In *Commission v Denmark* [1988], the ECJ accepted that environmental protection was another mandatory requirement. Danish legislation required that all beer and soft drinks sold in Denmark had to be packaged in re-usable containers. The European Commission challenged the legislation, alleging a breach of Art 28; the ECJ ruled that it was justifiable. In the event, the Court decided that the Danish legislation was unjustified, applying the proportionality test (see below), ie there were other means available to the Danish that would also protect the environment but in a way that was less restrictive on intra-State trade.

In *Aher-Waggon* [1998], concerning a challenge to German legislation that imposed limits on the decibel levels of planes, the Court again allowed protection of the environment as a derogation. In this case the Court went on to state that limiting aircraft noise emission was 'the most effective and convenient means of combating noise pollution'. Because the alternative – to carry out works in the vicinity of airports – would be difficult and expensive, the Court concluded that the German legislation was not disproportionate.

Maintenance of press diversity

In *Familiapress* [1997], Austrian legislation prohibited newspapers and magazines from incorporating crossword puzzles with cash prizes. This was designed to help smaller publishers to compete against much larger publishers who would otherwise be able to attract bigger readerships by offering bigger cash prizes, and thus maintain a diverse press. As German law contained no such prohibition, this law prevented German publishers who published magazines with prize competitions in them from selling their magazines in Austria. However, the Austrian law was held to be justifiable. The ECJ held that the maintenance of press diversity was a new mandatory requirement.

Proportionality

The requirements of proportionality (discussed above in the context of Art 30) also apply to the rule of reason. Many laws that might be justified, particularly on consumer protection grounds, are still found to be in breach of Art 28 because they are disproportionate (eg *Commission v Denmark*, considered above). Often the ECJ suggests clear labelling as an alternative method of protecting public health and/or the interests of the consumer. This was the result in *Walter Rau v De Smedt* [1982], considered above.

In *Commission v Germany* [1987], German law provided that the name 'bier' could only be used for products brewed using malted barley, hops, yeast and water. The use of other ingredients, such as rice or maize, while not precluding the marketing of a product in Germany, meant that it could not be sold as 'bier'. The European Commission alleged that this law was in breach of Art 28, because many imported beers did contain extra ingredients and thus could not be sold as 'bier'. The German government pleaded consumer protection. The ECJ disagreed. While it was legitimate to seek to 'enable consumers who attribute specific qualities to beers manufactured from particular raw materials to make their choice in the light of that consideration', prohibiting the name 'bier' was excessive. The Court suggested that 'the compulsory affixing of suitable labels giving the nature of the product sold' would suffice instead.

In *Clinique* [1994], German legislation prohibited the sale of cosmetics under misleading names, designations or presentations by which certain properties could be ascribed to properties which they did not in fact have. The German authorities regarded the name *Clinique* as one such misleading name – it could mislead consumers into thinking the product had medicinal qualities, as it evoked associations with the word 'clinic'. The consequence of this was that the manufacturers, Estée Lauder, had to repackage their product for the German market (it was renamed *Linique*) and advertise it differently everywhere else, obviously increasing their costs greatly. Eventually they challenged the German authorities under Art 28. The ECJ agreed that the German legislation was capable of infringing Art 28, but the German authorities responded with consumer protection. In the end, the Court held that the German rules were disproportionate: German consumers were sophisticated enough to appreciate that Clinique cosmetics did not have medicinal properties.

In *Commission v Spain and Italy* [2003], Italian and Spanish legislation banned the name 'chocolate' on packaging of chocolate products to which vegetable fats have been added. This affected British-made chocolate products, which traditionally contain vegetable fats. These could be sold in Italy and Spain only under the label 'chocolate substitute'. The European Commission launched actions on the basis that the legislation breached Art 28 because it forced chocolate producers in the UK (and some other Member States) to re-label their products for the Italian and Spanish markets. The Court agreed with the Commission. There was a breach of Art 28 because it was likely that Italian and Spanish consumers would regard products bearing the label 'chocolate substitute' as inferior, which would depress sales and thus restrict imports. The Court rejected Italy and Spain's defence of consumer protection. Although the Court acknowledged that it was important to draw consumers' attention to the fact that the chocolate products were not 'pure', this could be achieved by clearly indicating in the list of ingredients those vegetable fats that had been added.

MUTUAL RECOGNITION

In *Cassis de Dijon*, the ECJ – as well as creating the rule of reason principle – established a presumption that, once goods have been 'lawfully produced and marketed in one of the Member States', they may be imported into any other State. This has become known as the principle of 'mutual recognition'. The presumption may only be rebutted by evidence that the goods in question pose a threat to one of the heads of Art 30 or one of the mandatory requirements. The net result is to place the burden of proof on the authorities of the Member States seeking to justify their domestic legislation.

In practice, rebutting the presumption will not be easy to do. A successful rebuttal can be seen in *Muller* [1986]. French law restricted the use of E475, an emulsifying agent, in food. M, the manager of a baking company in France, had imported from Germany a cake and pastry mix called Phénix, which contained E475. He was prosecuted but claimed that the French law was in breach of Art 28. The ECJ agreed that the French law had the effect of restricting the importation of food from Germany, where the agent was freely available. However, the Court held that the law was justifiable under Art 30 on health grounds, taking into account the fact that consumption of bakery products was appreciably higher in France, particularly by children.

PROHIBITION OF DISCRIMINATORY TAXATION: ART 90

No Member State shall impose, directly or indirectly, on the products of the other Member States any internal taxation of any kind in excess of that imposed directly or indirectly on similar domestic products. Furthermore, no Member State shall impose on the products of other Member States any internal taxation of such nature as to afford indirect protection to other products.

Article 90 allows Member States the freedom to establish their own taxation system (often referred to as 'excise duties' in the UK) for any given product, provided there is no discrimination against imports, or indirect protection of domestic products. This can lead to significant differences in prices of the same goods from one Member State to another. For example, in the UK, the most heavily taxed goods are cigarettes, alcohol, perfume and petrol. Because cigarettes and alcohol are taxed at a much lower rate in France, the phenomenon of the 'booze cruise' – whereby UK nationals take the ferry across the English

Channel to France in order to buy those goods relatively cheaply – was created. Of course, under UK law – the Customs & Excise Management Act 1979 – individuals are not permitted to bring into the UK an unlimited amount of alcohol and cigarettes. HM Customs & Excise officers have to be vigilant in order to catch people bringing back consignments of those goods which are for commercial purposes, as opposed to personal use. Anyone bringing in goods for commercial purposes without payment of excise duty is potentially liable to have the goods forfeited – and to have their vehicle forfeited too. However, forfeiture of property in this way has been held to be a potential breach of both the free movement of goods under Art 28 EC and Art 1 of the First protocol of the European Convention of Human Rights (the right to property). Several cases in this area are discussed in Andrew Lidbetter's article, 'Customs, cars and Article 1 of the First protocol' (2004) 3 EHRLR 272.

'Tax'

The borderline between 'customs duties' (considered above) and 'taxes' may be difficult to draw. However, the ECJ has stated that Art 23 and Art 90 are mutually exclusive, so it is important to make the distinction clear. This is especially so given that many 'customs duties' are disguised as 'taxes'. A 'tax' was defined in *Commission v France* [1981] as one that related to:

A general system of internal duties applied systematically to categories of products in accordance with objective criteria irrespective of the origin of the products.

'Products of the other Member States'

Despite the clear implication of this phrase, the ECJ has held that the prohibition of discriminatory taxation must apply to goods manufactured or produced *outside* the EU, but which are in free circulation inside it (*Cooperativa Co-Frutta* [1987]).

Article 90(1): discrimination between imports and 'similar domestic products'

Where a system of taxation is *prima facie* non-discriminatory, but in effect discriminates against the imported product, it will still amount to a breach of Art 90(1). In *Humblot* [1985], the French government applied road tax on a sliding scale, with a significantly higher rate payable on cars exceeding 16 cv. No cars exceeding such capacity were made in France. H, a French taxpayer who imported a 36 cv Mercedes from Germany, sought repayment through the French courts of the excess tax. The ECJ held that such a system of taxation amounted to 'indirect' discrimination based on nationality, contrary to Art 90(1).

The ECJ had held that Art 90(1) must be construed broadly (*Commission v France* [1980]). It is not necessary that the imported and domestic products in question are *identical*. They need only be 'similar'. The test is whether the products 'have similar characteristics and meet the same needs from the point of view of consumers ... not according to whether they are strictly identical but whether their use is similar or comparable' (*Commission v Denmark* [1986]).

Most cases have arisen in the context of alcoholic drinks. In *John Walker & Sons* [1986], where different rates of tax were imposed by Denmark on fruit liqueur wines and whisky, the ECJ held that it was not enough for 'similarity' that both products contained alcohol. To be 'similar', the alcohol would have to be present in more or less equal measure. As whisky contained twice as much alcohol as fruit liqueur wines (40 per cent to 20 per cent), they were not similar products for the purposes of Art 90(1).

In *Commission v France* [1980], under French legislation, grain-based spirits (such as whisky and gin, which were largely imported) were subject to a much higher tax regime than fruit-based spirits (such as cognac and brandy), of which there was heavy French production. The European Commission, arguing that *all* spirits were 'similar', alleged a breach of Art 90(1). The French government argued that a distinction should be drawn between two classes of spirits: aperitifs and digestives. The former (including whisky and gin) were drunk, usually diluted with water or a mixer, before meals. The latter (including cognac and brandy) were beverages consumed, neat, at the end of a meal. Hence the two types were not 'similar'. The Court rejected this distinction. All the drinks could be consumed before, during or after meals or at any other time. The Court also rejected any distinction based on flavour. Although there were undoubtedly 'shades of difference' in the flavour of the various drinks, this criterion was 'too variable in time and space to supply by itself a sufficiently sound basis for distinction'. In the end, the Court concluded that it did not need to decide whether the drinks were 'similar' because it was 'impossible reasonably to contest that without exception they are in at least partial competition', and hence Art 90(2) applied instead.

Article 90(2): indirect protection of domestic products

For the purposes of Art 90(2), it is not even necessary for the products in question to be similar. Instead, it applies to 'all forms of indirect tax protection in the case of products which, without being similar within the meaning of Art 90(1), are nevertheless in competition, even partial, indirect or potential competition with each other' (*Cooperativa Co-Frutta* [1987]). It is thus much wider in scope than Art 90(1). Frequently, cases will be argued under Art 90(1) first. If the Court is not satisfied that the products are 'similar', it will then consider whether they are in competition.

Commission v UK [1983] concerned excise duties imposed on beer and wine in the UK in the late 1970s. Wine was being taxed at £3.25 per gallon while beer was being taxed at only 61p per gallon. The vast majority of wine consumed in the UK was imported (from France, Germany and Italy) while beer was predominantly domestically produced. The Commission alleged that the tax differential amounted to discrimination against imports. The UK claimed that the products, although both alcoholic drinks, were not 'similar'. The ECJ agreed that 'in view of the substantial differences between wine and beer' in terms of their different manufacturing processes and natural properties, the products were not 'similar'. There was therefore no breach of Art 90(1). However, the Court went on to hold that the UK was in breach of Art 90(2). The Court found that the effect of subjecting wine to a higher level of tax afforded protection to domestic beer production. The effect of the UK tax system was to 'stamp wine with the hallmarks of a luxury product which, in view of the tax burden which it bears, can scarcely constitute in the eyes of the consumer a genuine alternative to the typical domestically produced beverage'.

Cooperativa Co-Frutta [1987] is an example of the latter approach. A consumer tax was imposed in Italy on both domestic and imported bananas. As the domestic production was tiny, this in effect amounted to a tax on imports. No such charges were placed on other fresh fruit, such as pears, which were principally home-produced. The ECJ found this to be indirect protection of domestic fruit protection, and contrary to Art 90(2).

Finally, it should be noted that if there is found to be a protective effect in breach of Art 90(2) then the national legislation must be amended to remove the protective effect. However, provided this is achieved, it is not necessary for the rates of tax on the different but competing products to be equalised.

You should now be confident that you would be able to tick all of the boxes on the checklist at the beginning of this chapter. To check your knowledge of Free movement of goods why not visit the companion website and take the Multiple Choice Question test. Check your understanding of the terms and vocabulary used in this chapter with the flashcard glossary.

Putting it into practice . . .

8

Now that you've mastered the basics, you will want to put it all into practice. The Routledge-Cavendish Questions and Answers series provides an ideal opportunity for you to apply your understanding and knowledge of the law and to hone your essay-writing technique.

We've included one exam-style essay question, reproduced from the Routledge-Cavendish Questions and Answers series to give you some essential exam practice. The Q&A includes an answer plan and a fully worked model answer to help you recognise what examiners might look for in your answer.

QUESTION 1

'Although the European Parliament has limited powers, one cannot claim that the Community legislative process is devoid of democratic participation.'

Discuss.

Answer plan

This type of question has become very popular in recent years. This is largely due to developments which have affected the Parliament. The main points to cover in your answer are:

   powers and composition of the European Parliament;

   procedures of the Parliament; and

   role of the Parliament in the legislative process.

ANSWER

Since 1979, the Members of the European Parliament have been directly elected by their constituents in the Member States. Before that time, when the members were nominated by their respective governments, they had determined, as early as 1962, to call themselves a Parliament, even though the Treaty of Rome referred to them as an Assembly. Under Art 189, the European Parliament consists of 'representatives of the peoples of the States brought together in the Community'. It was not until the Single European Act 1986 that the Member States formally recognised the European Parliament by this name.

The European Parliament has certain characteristics similar to national parliaments, such as the UK Parliament at Westminster. There are a number of standing committees, which mirror the major policy areas of the Community. The committees carry out inquiries, hear evidence from experts and interested parties, including the Commission, and issue reports. In addition, parliamentary questions are an important element of control over the Commission. Under Art 197, the Commission must reply orally or in writing to questions put to it by MEPs. In fact, the Council and foreign ministers also take part in this process. It is common practice now for the President of the Council of Ministers to make a report to the Parliament at the end of his or her term as President.

There are two important powers associated with the European Parliament. The Treaty of Rome made the European Commission responsible to the European Parliament and is of little importance now. Once appointed by the Member States, the 25 Commissioners can only be removed by the European Parliament passing a censure motion by a two-thirds majority vote and an absolute majority of its Members. Such a motion, successfully passed, would force the resignation of the Commission. However, this power under Art 201 can only be used against the whole Commission and not against individual Commissioners. This power has never been exercised, although it has been threatened on a number of occasions. However, in order to avoid the motion of censure, the Commission did resign in March 1999, although its members remained in office until replaced by a new Commission in September of that year. With a view to making the institutions more democratic, the Treaty on European Union gave the European Parliament an important role in the process of appointing the President and Members of the Commission. This was achieved by the need for the Commission to be approved by Parliament in a vote of investiture.

Secondly, and perhaps the most important input that would be recognised as part of democratic participation, is the involvement of the European Parliament in making European laws, principally regulations and directives. There are many policy areas of the Treaty which give the Parliament the right to be consulted on proposed legislation. This is illustrated by the phrase, which is very familiar to any student of the Treaty, 'the Council, acting on a proposal from the Commission and after consulting the European Parliament, shall ...'. The normal procedure is that the proposal from the Commission is first considered by one of the Parliament's committees mentioned above, which will produce a report and a draft resolution. These then go to the full Parliament for debate before its opinion, including any suggested amendments, is sent to the Council.

As a result of this opinion, the Commission may modify its proposal, but there is no obligation on either the Council or the Commission to respond to it. However, whatever weight is given to the European Parliament's view, its right to be consulted must be respected. Failure to follow this procedural requirement may lead to the measure being declared invalid.

This happened in the cases of *Roquette v Council* and *Maizena v Council*, both reported in 1980. An interesting discussion took place in these cases with regard to what extent this requirement gave power to the Parliament to block legislation. Is the requirement that the European Parliament should be asked for its opinion or must it actually give it? The Council argued that if the latter was true, then the Parliament could delay legislation indefinitely by the simple expedient of not giving an opinion. The ECJ interpreted the requirement under the Treaty to mean that the Parliament has to give its opinion. However, it left open the question of what would happen if the Parliament were to be deliberately obstructive and the Council wished to go ahead with the legislation. Such an impasse has not yet occurred.

It is understandable that in these circumstances, where its opinion carried limited importance to the Council, the European Parliament was often called 'a mere talking shop' by national politicians. With the direct elections of 1979, MEPs saw themselves as the true representatives of their constituents and increasingly called for an active part in the legislative process. This was given by Arts 6 and 7 of the Single European Act 1986, which amended the original Treaty. This required a co-operation procedure to be operative in some instances, but by no means all, where the Treaty required the Parliament to be consulted. The main difference is that in theory, the views of the European Parliament carry more importance, although in practice, this change may not be so significant. When the Council receives a proposal from the Commission, it adopts a 'common position', which is sent to the European Parliament. The Parliament now has three months in which to act. If Parliament rejects the common position, the Council can adopt the proposal only by unanimity. If Parliament wishes to amend the proposal, such amendments are sent back to the Commission for consideration. These amendments may be adopted, but there is no obligation on the Commission to do so. The proposal is then sent back to the Council along with any parliamentary amendments it had not accepted and the reasons for this refusal. The Council can accept the amended proposal by a qualified majority or it can amend it by adopting its own amendments or those proposed by the Parliament. This has to be done by a unanimous vote in the Council.

In practice, the co-operation procedure appears to grant the European Parliament very little extra power. It provides for a possible alliance between a Member State and the Parliament in the sense that the Council of Ministers would not have the unanimity to overrule amendments. But does this give more authority to the Member State or the European Parliament? Also, the requirement on the Commission under the co-operation procedure to consider the Parliament's amendments and to give reasons for not adopting them makes a legal requirement of something which was a matter of practice before. In fact, perhaps the most significant increase in the Parliament's powers brought about by the Single European Act is the requirement for its approval in relation to the admission of new members to the Community or the conclusion of association agreements with third countries. Under the Act, the European Parliament thus has a veto in such matters.

However, the big step forward in democratic involvement was the introduction of the co-decision procedure in the Treaty on European Union. Under this procedure, Parliament shares the decision making power equally with the Council. If Parliament decides to reject the proposal, it cannot be adopted by the Council. To avoid this deadlock, a conciliation committee is convened with a membership drawn from the European Parliament, the Council and the Commission. If agreement is still not reached, the European Parliament can reject the proposal definitively. The Treaty of Amsterdam 1997 simplified the procedure to make it more efficient in Art 251.

An aspect of democratic participation which has always been considered important in any parliament is the involvement of elected representatives in the setting of expenditure and income levels, that is, a budget. Although it is the President of the European Parliament alone who has the power to adopt the budget, the procedure for the Community budget is rather complex and has been varied on several occasions. The effect of these changes has been to transfer certain powers from the Council to the Parliament.

The European Parliament's right to make changes in the budget depends on the distinction between expenditure which is 'compulsory' and that which is 'non-compulsory'. Compulsory expenditure covers that expenditure which is committed under Treaty provisions or Community legislation. The main example is expenditure on the common agricultural policy. Parliament can only propose modifications to this category of expenditure, thus giving the Council the final say in such matters. However, non-compulsory expenditure, which includes all expenditure which is not the inevitable consequence of Community legislation, can be amended by the majority of MEPs voting in favour of such proposals. This expenditure includes the Community social policy, regional and industrial policies, and accounts for about 42 per cent of the total Community budget. For this type of expenditure, it is the European Parliament which has final control. Therefore, although the Parliament does have some powers of approval as far as the budget is concerned, these are weak with regard to compulsory expenditure, which comprises the majority of the total budget.

However, in 1975, the European Parliament was given increased powers in relation to the Community budget by a conciliation procedure. The aim of these powers is to give the Parliament more effective participation in the budgetary process by seeking agreement between the Parliament and the Council of Ministers. If the Parliament refuses to pass the budget as presented to it by the Council, a number of important consequences follow. First, the budget cannot be implemented, which has implications for the expenditure level of the Community (limited to one-12th of the previous year's budget per month). Secondly, a 'conciliation committee', consisting of the Council and representatives of the European Parliament, is established to try to resolve the disagreement. The European Commission assists the work of the committee.

Ultimately, the Parliament may reject the budget outright under Art 272 of the EC Treaty by a vote cast by a two-thirds majority of its members. This has now happened on four occasions, in 1980 by the newly directly elected Parliament, eager to use its budgetary powers, and in 1982, 1986 and 1988. Although it may reject it, the Parliament cannot increase the total amount of the budget beyond the maximum rate of increase set by the Commission, unless the alteration is agreed by the Council. The disagreement is generally, therefore, centred on the distribution of the budget. Such disagreements sometimes erupt into the public domain and have been subject to proceedings before the ECJ, as in *EC Council v European Parliament* in 1986. In 1988, in an attempt to improve the budgetary procedure, an institutional agreement was entered into by the Council, Commission and the European Parliament. While recognising the varying competencies of the institutions in the budgetary field, it fixed new rules for co-operation between the institutions. However, the Council successfully obtained the annulment of the adoption of the budget by the European Parliament because the Parliament had exceeded its powers regarding compulsory expenditure (*Council of the European Union v European Parliament* [1995]).

The normal authority of a parliament is that the national government is dependent upon confidence and continued support to remain in office. There is no such relationship between the European Parliament and the main political decision-making body in the Community, the Council of Ministers. The ministers who form the Council are representing their national governments, who in turn must retain the support of his national parliaments. Therefore, any vote cast by a minister at Council meetings must be supported by their national parliament. Is this the main democratic control over European legislation? Are the national Members of Parliament, representing the same constituents as the MEPs, exercising democratic control? In theory, this could be possible, at least for major issues. However, it has one major drawback, in that the national parliaments rarely have the procedures or time necessary for clear debate of issues before they are discussed and agreed at the Council of Ministers. Although attempts are being made to ensure better information and debate in national parliaments of European issues, this is not happening at the moment. The only really genuine and consistent debate takes place in the European Parliament, but what authority does that have? As indicated above, it has some important powers, and there is pressure for these to be extended. Since the TEU, both the Treaty of Amsterdam and the Treaty of Nice have extended the area of EU policy subject to the co-decision procedure. The Constitution Treaty 2004 proposed to increase the scope of the co-decision procedure and give more involvement to national parliaments but it has not yet been ratified by all Member States.

Each Routledge-Cavendish Q&A contains fifty essay and problem-based questions on topics commonly found on exam papers, complete with answer plans and fully worked model answers. For further examination practice, visit the Routledge-Cavendish website or your local bookstore today!